Harvard Business Re

Arm yourself with the advice you need to succeed on the job, from the most trusted brand in business. Packed with how-to essentials from leading experts, the HBR Guides provide smart answers to your most pressing work challenges.

The titles include:

HBR Guide for Women at Work
HBR Guide to Being More Productive
HBR Guide to Better Business Writing
HBR Guide to Building Your Business Case
HBR Guide to Buying a Small Business
HBR Guide to Changing Your Career
HBR Guide to Coaching Employees
HBR Guide to Data Analytics Basics for Managers
HBR Guide to Dealing with Conflict
HBR Guide to Delivering Effective Feedback
HBR Guide to Emotional Intelligence
HBR Guide to Finance Basics for Managers
HBR Guide to Getting the Mentoring You Need
HBR Guide to Getting the Right Work Done
HBR Guide to Leading Teams
HBR Guide to Making Better Decisions
HBR Guide to Making Every Meeting Matter
HBR Guide to Managing Strategic Initiatives
HBR Guide to Managing Stress at Work

HBR Guide to
Setting Your Strategy

HARVARD BUSINESS REVIEW PRESS

Boston, Massachusetts

Library of Congress Cataloging-in-Publication Data

Title: HBR guide to setting your strategy.
Other titles: Harvard Business Review guide to setting your strategy | Harvard business review guides.
Description: Boston, Massachusetts : Harvard Business Review Press, [2020] | Series: Harvard Business Review guides | Includes index.
Identifiers: LCCN 2020012315 (print) | LCCN 2020012316 (ebook) | ISBN 9781633698925 (paperback) | ISBN 9781633698932 (ebook)
Subjects: LCSH: Strategic planning. | Business planning.
Classification: LCC HD30.28 .H3935 2020 (print) | LCC HD30.28 (ebook) | DDC 658.4/012—dc23
LC record available at https://lccn.loc.gov/2020012315
LC ebook record available at https://lccn.loc.gov/2020012316

ISBN: 978-1-63369-892-5
eISBN: 978-1-63369-893-2

What You'll Learn

Every company needs a strategy, one that will position it to grow over the long term. But charting such a path forward can be challenging, especially if your industry is facing new entrants, frequent disruption, or increased regulation. Your strategy must account for where you're competing, the customers you are targeting, what you aim to offer, and what your people need to succeed. And it must be communicated in a way that ensures buy-in from stakeholders—especially your employees. Otherwise, execution may fall flat.

Whether you are revising a strategy you already have or formulating your startup's strategy for the first time, this guide will provide you with practical tips and advice to help you define a strategy that will give your company a competitive edge, test it to ensure it will work, communicate it to others and execute it, and adapt it as needed.

You'll learn to:

- Understand the basics of strategy, implementation, and execution

- Consider the predictability and malleability of your industry

- Organize a more productive strategy offsite

- Recognize who your stakeholders are, what their needs are, and what you want from them

- Consider where you'll play and how to win in crafting your strategy

- Build purpose and creativity into your strategy

- Think in the long term, rather than in annual—or quarterly—cycles

- Identify the capabilities you need to ensure success

- Test your strategy before implementing it

- Communicate your strategy to your team by defining what you *won't* be doing

- Evaluate and adjust your strategy over time

Contents

Contents

SECTION FOUR

Test Your Strategic Choices

Get the Strategy You Need—Now

What's your competitive advantage? Who are your key customers and stakeholders? How will you respond to disruption in the marketplace? Do you have the capabilities in place to succeed, and are your people aligned? Are you planning for the future—the right way?

If these questions make you sweat, you're not alone. Setting a strategy that will help your organization or business unit succeed while responding to new competitors and changes to your industry is daunting. Assessing potential threats while creating new ways to grow is a difficult balance. Choose the wrong strategy, and you can stumble—or worse, go out of business. But find the right strategy and you can stand out to your customers and last for years to come.

But where do you start? And what do you need to think about? How do you decide where and how to compete, gain buy-in from your stakeholders and employees, and ensure your strategy is executed properly?

Whether you're retooling your organization's existing strategy, creating one from scratch as a startup, or outlining a plan for your specific business unit, this guide will help you think about your business in the right way to create a strategy specific to your needs. You'll discover questions to ask and advice to follow to define a well-thought-out strategy, test it before implementation, and communicate it effectively for others to execute.

The Benefits of Smart Strategy

There's no one, universal definition of strategy, but for the purposes of this book, you can think of strategy in the way that Stephen Bungay, Director of the Ashridge Strategic Management Centre, states in chapter 2: "Strategy is about what we are going to do now in order to shape the future to our advantage."

Setting a strategy gives you an active role in planning for your company's future. Without it, too many of your actions will be focused on the short term—reacting to every potential threat, meeting goals that may not have long-term impact, and focusing too much on the day-to-day operations and problem solving. What's more, without an eye on the big picture, you may miss the larger shifts in your industry—shifts that require early planning in order to respond and thrive.

Having a clearly thought-out and communicated strategy also allows decision making across your organization to align, so everyone is moving in the same direction. Leaders and employees alike can then prioritize the correct projects and initiatives, focus on the right metrics, and invest in the most crucial areas. And they can make smart changes in response to new competitors or stakeholder interests.

And it isn't just organizations that need a strategy. Business units also need to have such principles and fundamentals in place. While your company may decide that setting up a new office in Tokyo to expand its international presence is part of its global strategy, your business unit may then need to assess if its products and offerings need to change amid new competitors in the Japanese market. Either way, understanding the steps to setting a strategy, communicating it to your employees, and executing it will be critical for leaders at any level.

What This Book Will Do

From Michael Porter's five forces to agile approaches, how we've thought about strategy has transformed and shifted over time. But this book will not focus on any one specific school of thought. Rather, it will explore the *practice* of setting your strategy, so you can work with your leadership team to formulate the approach that works best for your unique capabilities, circumstances, and industry.

This guide will help you set a strategy for your organization or business unit by explaining the basics of what strategy is, helping you to lay the foundation for strategic discussions, walking you through what to think about when formulating your strategy, testing it before implementation, communicating it to your employees, and finally executing and learning from it.

- **What is strategy?** The first section in this book helps you understand the basics of strategy, starting with the difference between strategy, implementation, and execution, and how each relate to both corporate and business strategy. It then debunks five common myths about strategy and explains how strategies, objectives, and actions differ, so you'll understand how these work together in your strategic planning sessions.

- **Laying the foundation.** Before you lead a strategy discussion, you and your leadership team must have some basic understanding in place. The first two chapters outline four strategic styles that correspond with the predictability and malleability of your industry and describe a variety of approaches to making strategic decisions. Chapter 6 looks at the specifics of the strategy offsite, offering tips and advice to ensure a productive conversation. The last chapter in this section helps you think carefully about your stakeholders, understanding both what you want from them and what they want from you, so you can take that into account in your strategy formulation.

- **Develop your strategy.** Once you've established the basics, you're ready to dive into your strategic discussions. The first chapter of section 3 provides approaches to think about strategy creatively— through contrast, combination, constraint, and context. Next, Roger Martin, author of *Playing to Win*, provides five key questions to consider, what he calls the "strategy choice cascade." In chapter 10, you'll learn about common competitive threats, so you can face potential uncertainty as you develop a path forward, and in chapter 11, futurist Amy Webb explains how to think about the long term—looking long past the standard five years ahead. Strategy should always be changing, though, especially as fast-growing platform companies have more and more influence in many industries. Chapter 12 helps you understand how these companies may affect your business and whether (and how) you should adjust your approach. The section closes with a look at purpose, and how you can incorporate it into your strategy.

- **Test your strategic choices.** It's hardly feasible to assume that a new strategy will work seamlessly. Before you move your plan forward, you need to test it, and section 4 helps you to do just that. Chapter 14 provides ways to pressure-test your strategy, including helping you to build situational awareness, taking an outside-in perspective, and war-gaming. The next chapter helps you identify where you may be falling victim to your own cognitive biases in your strategic decision making. Then, you'll assess what capabilities you require to be successful by identifying what your organization or business unit should do differently, and defining how to build the skills, knowledge, and processes you need to carry out these changes.

Last, you'll look at your organization or team's strategic alignment to make sure that your people are able to support the strategy.

- **Communicate your strategy.** Any plans you make will go nowhere if your people don't understand them. Communication—and communication in the right way—remains critical to successful execution. Section 5 begins by outlining how to explain your strategy to your people, particularly given that with a new approach often comes change. Next, you'll discover how to help your team understand your strategy and its priorities by contrasting what they *will* be working on with what they *won't*. Last, you'll learn how to conduct these conversations across cultures, especially since diverse talent can have different points of view on competition and the market.

- **Execute the strategy and learn from it.** The final section in this book helps you to execute and adapt your strategy as necessary. The first chapter explores how strategy and execution are linked, and explains how to examine gaps in execution, learn from them, and adjust your strategy accordingly. The next chapter identifies common execution traps to avoid. You'll then learn the risk of putting too much focus on metrics—specifically quarterly numbers—and how that can take your strategy off course. Finally, the concluding chapter of the book emphasizes that becoming an expert strategist won't happen overnight—it requires practice. Roger Martin provides tips for how you can improve your development process as you revisit and adjust your strategy, so over time you can become a more confident and more accomplished strategist.

While the steps outlined in this book are not rigid in their order, it's important not to skip over any of them. Without laying the right foundation, your discussions are unlikely to prove fruitful. Without testing, you're likely to stumble in unforeseen ways. And without effective communication, it's highly unlikely you'll see your strategy executed well, whether you're leading the entire organization or a business unit.

Above all, it's important to remember that a strategy is never static. Your plans will require frequent assessment, adjustment, and refining. According to Martin, "competitors don't wait for your annual strategy cycle to attack, customers don't wait for your annual strategy cycle to shift their preferences, and new technology doesn't wait for your annual strategy cycle to leapfrog yours."[1] Lead your company into the future by thinking about your strategy regularly—starting now.

NOTE

1. Roger L. Martin, "Three Quick Ways to Improve Your Strategy-Making," hbr.org, May 22, 2014 (product #H00TEP).

What Is Strategy?

CHAPTER 1

Defining Strategy, Implementation, and Execution

by Ken Favaro

It is striking how much confusion there is between strategy, implementation, and execution. Is "strategy" a matter of making choices about where we want to go, where we play and how we win, of setting goals and actions, about how we create and capture economic value over time? Does it include creating solutions to unforeseen problems and running with unexpected opportunities? Is "getting things done" what we mean by

---

Adapted from content posted on hbr.org, March 31, 2015 (product #H01YRY).

implementation or execution? Do you "execute" or "implement" a strategy? And can you separate these from strategy formation?

For strategy wonks like me, thinking about the definitions of these ideas provides endless fascination. For many business leaders, however, I find that the semantics matter a lot less. And that's too bad because the semantics should matter. There are meaningful distinctions between strategy, implementation, and execution that are helpful to running a company or business in the real world. Ignoring, blurring, or getting them wrong creates sloppy thinking, deciding, and doing at all levels of an organization.

Let's start with strategy. As I understand the term, strategy consists of two categories: corporate strategy and business unit strategy. Corporate strategy consists of CEOs and top executives making just three basic choices:

- What should be the capabilities that distinguish the company?

- What should be the company's comparative advantage in adding value to its individual businesses?

- What businesses should the company be in?

These are the fundamental choices that constitute a *corporate* strategy, and they should frame and guide all the decisions that a company's corporate executives, functions, and staff make every day, including how they run the place, what they buy, what markets they enter, how they measure success, and so on.

For a business unit, there are also three key decisions that cannot be delegated by its leader. They are different but no less fundamental:

- Who should be the customers who define our target market?

- What should be the value proposition that differentiates our products and services with those customers?

- What should be the capabilities that make our business better than any other in delivering that value proposition?

These are the choices that a *business* strategy comprises, and they should drive the decisions a business unit's management team, functions, and staff make every day, including pricing, R&D, where to manufacture, and many more.

This brings me to implementation. Implementing a strategy consists of all the decisions and activities required to put the two sets of strategic choices I've just described into effect. If the corporation has the capabilities, enterprise advantage, and business portfolio it wants, its strategy is implemented. If the unit has the customers, value proposition, and skills it has chosen to have, its strategy is also fully implemented.

Of course, almost by definition, a strategy can never actually be fully implemented because everything that you necessarily assumed when formulating it—about customers, technology, regulation, competitors, and so on—is in a constant state of flux. CEOs and their business unit leaders must continuously evolve their strategies (i.e., those fundamental choices listed above) if they are to remain relevant and competitive. And if that's the case, there will always be a gap between where their companies are and what their strategies call for. Closing that gap is "implementation." Thus, developing and implementing strategy are running almost continuously in parallel rather than in sequence.

What, then, is execution? I define the term as the decisions and activities you undertake in order to turn your implemented strategy into commercial success. To achieve "execution excellence" is to realize the best possible results a strategy and its implementation will allow.

To understand what this means, let's say that Netflix has made a corporate strategy choice to enter the content business and to exit the mail order business. Once Netflix is in the content business and out of the mail order business, that "strategy" (or that part of its strategy) is implemented. Now, Netflix leaders must set goals and plans for the content business, establish the right incentives, create a motivational, purpose-driven mission statement, and more. All leaders need such activities to realize great results from their companies within the context of an implemented strategy. This is execution.

Strategy, implementation, and execution are three coincident determinants of a company or business unit's ultimate output—its results—that are very difficult to parse into their individual effects. When we see a company or business unit producing poor results over multiple years, no one can say for sure whether that's due to poor strategy, implementation, or execution. But in my experience, it's very difficult to implement a poor strategy well and doubly difficult to produce excellent results with a poor strategy that's being poorly implemented. (Having a great corporate or business strategy is no guarantee of great results either; you still have to implement and execute well.)

The distinctions I make above are not between thinking and doing, deciding and acting, or planning and producing. All of these kinds of activities are involved in strategy, implementation, and execution. Does that make them the same thing? Absolutely not. They each involve very different specific activities, tools, and people. And when business leaders conflate strategy, implementation, and execution, they usually end up with a lot of the trappings of running a modern-day company or business unit—such as goals and targets; plans and initiatives; and mission, vision, and purpose statements—but very little actual strategy, implementation, or execution.

Lim Chow Kiat, CEO of Singapore's GIC, says that for his organization "nomenclature is destiny . . . We are meticulous about word choice . . . The wrong words can corrode, if not corrupt, our [business]." I agree. Leaders do themselves a great disservice by not being more thoughtful about what they mean when they say strategy, implementation, and execution.

Ken Favaro is lead principal of act2, an independent adviser to CEOs and their teams and boards based in Bronxville, New York. He is the author of the forthcoming book *Strategy 101*.

CHAPTER 2

Five Myths About Strategy

by Stephen Bungay

There are lies, there are big lies, and then there are myths. And myths are the worst of the three.

Unless you have sealed yourself off in a social media echo chamber, lies are easy to spot. Except, that is, when the lie is a big one. People hearing or reading big lies start to doubt themselves and think "maybe I have got things completely wrong." That's why politicians and propagandists tell big lies. They're not trying to assert a truth so much as sow doubt and confusion about what is true. That's bad, but a smart person can resist a big lie by looking at the evidence at hand.

Adapted from content posted on hbr.org, April 19, 2019 (product #H04WWB).

Myths present a different, subtler trap, which is what makes even smart people fall for them. They are seductive because they are based on a half-truth. That element of truth is what allows them to become established as myths, and they do not immediately lead you astray if you start to act on them. It's only with the passage of time that you realize that you've made a mistake, but by then your wrong choices can't be unmade and the damage is done.

We encounter myths in most realms of human endeavor and the discipline of strategic thinking is no exception. Here are five of the most pernicious ones I've encountered in a long career studying strategy and advising companies about it:

Myth 1: Strategy Is About the Long Term

Why it's plausible

In some industries, the basis of competition can remain unchanged for decades, and leaders who stick to their strategy through downturns as well as upturns and ignore surface noise do very well.

Why it's wrong

It is precisely when long-held assumptions about an industry are challenged that strategic changes happen. And you will need to make those changes very quickly. Thinking about strategy as a long-term commitment can blind you to that need. Strategy is not about the long term or the short term, but about the *fundamentals* of how the business works: the sources of value creation, the drivers of the cost to deliver it, and the basis of competition. To get a grip on strategy, we do not need to lengthen the time horizon of our thinking but its *depth*. Far from being about things we are going to do in the future, strategy is about what we are going to do *now* in order to shape the future to our advantage.

Myth 2: Disruptors Change Strategy All the Time

Why it's plausible

It looks as if Amazon and the platform giants like Google and Facebook keep changing strategy because they use the massive amounts of cash they generate to innovate, bringing out new products and services every year. Innovation is easily confused with a change in strategic direction, and sometimes it does indeed trigger such a change.

Why it's wrong

In the case of Amazon and the rest of Big Tech, most of the innovative new products and services reflect a single, consistent strategy, one that's been familiar to business people since at least the 1960s. That's when Bruce Henderson, the founder of Boston Consulting Group (BCG), observed that in many businesses, costs decline by a predictable amount with every doubling of cumulative volume. The implication was that by pricing ahead in anticipation of those cost declines, a company could sacrifice current margins to gain share, achieve market leadership, and then reap the gains. The strategy was captured in the imperative: "Cut price and add capacity." That's basically what today's platform businesses are doing—though they do use more jazzy vocabulary like "blitzscaling" or "hypergrowth" and add some twists. For today's platform businesses for instance, the imperative could be called: "Give it away and add users." But it's just a more radical version of a strategy that's more than half a century old.

Myth 3: Competitive Advantage Is Dead

Why it's plausible

There is evidence that the time period over which advantage can be sustained is shortening, which suggests that achieving defensibility is harder, which in turn implies that barriers are more flimsy and easier to surmount. One market observer notes that average tenure in the S&P 500 had fallen from 33 years in 1964 to 24 years by 2016 and is forecast to shrink to just 12 years by 2027.[1]

Why it's wrong

Reports of the death of competitive advantage are vastly exaggerated. The competitive advantages of Amazon, Alphabet, Apple, Facebook, and Microsoft are so massive and the barriers to overcoming them so high that public discussion of them revolves around the use of regulation to break them up to reduce their power. In a very short time, it has become hard to imagine how market forces alone could tame them. The full truth is not that competitive advantage is dead but that you need to rely on multiple advantages rather than just the one. And part of the reason that Amazon and these other companies will be hard to unseat is that they have realized this. They are not betting on building a single big wall but on building lots of smaller ones.

Myth 4: You Don't Really Need a Strategy; You Just Need to Be Agile

Why it's plausible

Agile firms—especially startups—are always turning on a dime, and they certainly don't seem to be following any kind of plan. Easy enough, then, to assume that what you see an agile firm doing—acting at high speed, maintaining a high tempo, being highly responsive—is all there is.

Why it's wrong

Agility is not a strategy. It is a *capability*, a very valuable one that has immediate operational benefits but that cannot permanently affect a firm's competitive position unless there is a strategist making the right decisions about where to direct that capability. And the seeming absence of a plan doesn't mean that successful startups don't have strategies. A strategy is not a plan; it is a framework for decision making, a set of guiding principles which can be applied as the situation evolves. And most startups fail because being able to turn on a dime doesn't mean that you'll turn in the right direction. Successful startups actually do a lot of hard thinking

21

about fundamentals, questioning and testing basic assumptions with a rigor that incumbents would do well to emulate. Startups have to, because their resources are extremely scarce. If they don't have a coherent strategy, they will make poor resource allocation decisions, and for them that will not mean a fall in earnings, but death.

Myth 5: You Need a Digital Strategy

Why it's plausible

Digital technology is a way of collecting, storing, and using information, and information is everywhere. In its early stages, it enabled us to do what we did already rather better. Then it enabled us to do it a lot better. Then it enabled us to do things we had never done before. Now the possibilities are exhilarating but also confusing. When people feel confused they look for a way of sorting things out, making sense of them, and deciding what to do. Hence the call for a digital strategy.

Why it's wrong

A company is an organism, and if you try to optimize the parts you will suboptimize the whole. You don't want a strategy for digital, IT, finance, HR, or anything else— just a strategy for the entire business. So don't imagine you can develop a strategy for the digital part of your business and leave the rest alone. Digital technology and the more specific technologies to which it gives rise fundamentally change the sources of customer value and the cost of delivering it. The way to address digital is to think through and lay out all the fundamental assumptions you have about how your company works and ask yourself if they are still valid. And that's what strategy has always been about.

In our uncertain world, fundamentals are changing so we need to think about them and whether they are valid in the short or long term. Think how you can deploy the capabilities you have and build new ones you need to defend your competitive position. Add them in layers to create barriers. Be clear about what will make a difference so that you can make rapid resource allocation decisions. Be on the lookout for the emergence of unexpected events at the customer interface that point to opportunities that can be deliberately exploited. Play to win the short games that will enable you to prevail in the long ones. Think deep to act fast. Strategy is still what it has always been: the art of taking action under the pressure of the most difficult conditions.

Stephen Bungay is a director of the Ashridge Strategic Management Centre in London. He is the author of *The Art of Action: How Leaders Close the Gaps Between Plans, Actions and Results*.

NOTE

1. Scott D. Anthony, S. Patrick Viguerie, Evan I. Schwartz, and John Van Landeghem, "2018 Corporate Longevity Forecast: Creative Destruction Is Accelerating," Innosight, https://www.innosight.com/insight/creative-destruction/.

CHAPTER 3

Your Strategic Plans Probably Aren't Strategic, or Even Plans

by Graham Kenny

It happens all the time: A group of managers get together at a resort for two days to hammer out a "strategic plan." Done and dusted, they all head home. But *have* they produced a plan with a strategy?

At the start of my public seminars on strategic planning I ask attendees, who rank from board members and CEOs to middle management, to write down an

---

Adapted from content posted on hbr.org, April 6, 2018 (product #H049N3).

example of a strategy on a sheet of paper. They look at me quizzically at first as they realize that this is a tough assignment. I reassure them that this is indeed a hard question, and they plow ahead.

The results are always astonishing to me and them. Here are some of the responses from the list I received at my most recent session: actions ("launch a new service," "review our suitability to the retirement business"), activities ("marketing our products through the right channels"), objectives ("achieve $100 million net revenue"), and broad descriptions of what goes on ("planning process from beginning to end of product," "working for your stakeholders").

Sorry folks, but not even one of these responses is a strategy.

Unfortunately, while C-suite executives talk "strategy" they're often confused about what it means. Why this confusion? The problem starts with the word itself— a scarily misunderstood concept in management and board circles. The most basic mix-up is between "objective," "strategy," and "action." (I see this frequently in published strategic plans as well.) Grasp this, I tell my audience, and your day will be well spent.

An "objective" is something you're trying to achieve— a marker of the *success of the organization.* At the other end of the spectrum is "action." This occurs at the *individual level*—a level that managers are presented with day after day. So naturally when they think "strategy" they focus on what they *do.* But this isn't strategy either. "Strategy" takes place between these two at the *organization level* and managers can't "feel" that in the same way. It's abstract. CEOs have an advantage here because only they have a total view of the organization.

The key to strategy is that it's the positioning of one business against others—GM against Ford and Toyota, for example. What exactly is positioning? It's placement on the strategic factors relevant to each key stakeholder group.

An organization exists as part of a system composed of transactions between itself and its key stakeholders such as customers, employees, suppliers, and shareholders. Organizations differ in the detail of these sets, depending on the complexity of the industry in which they're located. (For more on stakeholders, see chapter 7.)

The task of a strategic planning team is to produce positions on these factors that deliver value to the organization's key stakeholders *and* meet the objectives of the organization. Let's go back to our seminar list and take one of the responses: "achieve $100 million net revenue." This is an objective, rather than a strategy. A strategy serves an objective by providing a position on the relevant strategic factors—in this case for customers.

Let's say the strategic planning team identifies "price" as one strategic factor. In this case let's make the business Dan Murphy's, Australia's largest liquor retailer with a national footprint. It has stated its position on this factor unequivocally: "Lowest liquor price guaranteed. In the unlikely event that a customer finds a lower price, we'll beat it on the spot." This is that company's position on price. Alternatively, let's look at Toyota. A strategic factor relevant to the same type of objective for customers is "safety." By reviewing its materials, we can construe the company's position on this as: Safety is paramount, and our cars are among the most advanced, reliable, and safest on the road.

Now to ensure implementation, a strategic planning team must identify some *project- or program-level* actions. McDonald's had to do this when on "product range" it took this position: *Traditional meal range but with an increased emphasis on salad items and with the option for customers to design their own burgers. Periodic special offerings to spur customer interest.* You can envision the high-level actions that might follow such as: Design a training program for all staff in made-to-order food handling procedures.

If you take a helicopter view of the process I've outlined, you can see that it involves system design. Each key stakeholder group is taken in turn to work out what an organization wants from it (an objective) and what the key stakeholder wants from it (strategic factors)—for example, customers want effective performance on factors such as price and customer service. The strategic planning team must then decide on the organization's position on these factors (strategy). This will be conditioned, of course, by customer research. Having done this, key stakeholder by key stakeholder, the next step is to ensure congruence—a fit between employee relations and customer relations, customer relations and supplier relations, and so on—in system design.

My experience in working with clients over many years is that executive teams fail to approach strategic planning from a system-design perspective. A major cause of this is that managers within these teams approach the task from their own functional-management view, for example, finance, HR, marketing, operations. Consequently, they think "action" when they mean to think "strategy." Taking a stakeholder approach to strategic planning induces managers to raise their thinking to the organization level.

Remember: Strategic planning is a journey, not a project. Plans require ongoing adjustment. Yes, kickstart yours with a two-day retreat. But never end it there.

Graham Kenny, CEO of Strategic Factors, is a recognized expert in strategy. He is passionate about helping managers, executives, and boards create successful organizations in the private, public, and not-for-profit sectors. He does this through seminars and workshops on strategy and performance measurement; through keynote speaking; by working with managers to develop their business strategy and performance scorecards; and by publishing books, articles, and manuals. You can connect to or follow him on LinkedIn.

Lay the Foundation

CHAPTER 4

Your Strategy Needs a Strategy

**by Martin Reeves, Claire Love,
and Philipp Tillmanns**

The oil industry holds relatively few surprises for strategists. Things change, of course, sometimes dramatically, but in relatively predictable ways. Planners know, for instance, that global supply will rise and fall as geopolitical forces play out and new resources are discovered and exploited. They know that demand will rise and fall with incomes, GDPs, weather conditions, and the like. Because these factors are outside companies' and their competitors' control and barriers to entry are so high, no one is really in a position to change the game much. A

Reprinted from *Harvard Business Review*, September 2012 (product #R1209E).

company carefully marshals its unique capabilities and resources to stake out and defend its competitive position in this fairly stable firmament.

The internet software industry would be a nightmare for an oil industry strategist. Innovations and new companies pop up frequently, seemingly out of nowhere, and the pace at which companies can build—or lose—volume and market share is head-spinning. A major player like Microsoft or Google or Facebook can, without much warning, introduce some new platform or standard that fundamentally alters the basis of competition. In this environment, competitive advantage comes from reading and responding to signals faster than your rivals do, adapting quickly to change, or capitalizing on technological leadership to influence how demand and competition evolve.

Clearly, the kinds of strategies that would work in the oil industry have practically no hope of working in the far less predictable and far less settled arena of internet software. And the skill sets that oil and software strategists need are worlds apart as well, because they operate on different time scales, use different tools, and have very different relationships with the people on the front lines who implement their plans. Companies operating in such dissimilar competitive environments should be planning, developing, and deploying their strategies in markedly different ways. But all too often, our research shows, they are not.

That is not for want of trying. Responses from a recent BCG survey of 120 companies around the world in 10 major industry sectors show that executives are well aware of the need to match their strategy-making processes to the specific demands of their competitive environments. Still, the survey found, in practice many rely instead on approaches that are better suited to predictable, stable environments, even when their own environments are known to be highly volatile or mutable.

What's stopping these executives from making strategy in a way that fits their situation? We believe they lack a systematic way to go about it—a strategy for making strategy. Here we present a simple framework that divides strategy planning into four styles according to how predictable your environment is and how much power you have to change it. Using this framework, corporate leaders can match their strategic style to the particular conditions of their industry, business function, or geographic market.

How you set your strategy constrains the kind of strategy you develop. With a clear understanding of the strategic styles available and the conditions under which each is appropriate, more companies can do what we have found that the most successful are already doing—deploying their unique capabilities and resources to better capture the opportunities available to them.

Finding the Right Strategic Style

Strategy usually begins with an assessment of your industry. Your choice of strategic style should begin there as well. Although many industry factors will play into the strategy you actually formulate, you can narrow down your options by considering just two critical factors: *predictability* (How far into the future and how accurately can you confidently forecast demand, corporate performance, competitive dynamics, and market expectations?) and *malleability* (To what extent can you or your competitors influence those factors?).

Put these two variables into a matrix, and four broad strategic styles—which we label *classical, adaptive, shaping,* and *visionary*—emerge. (See figure 4-1.) Each style is associated with distinct planning practices and is best suited to one environment. Too often strategists conflate predictability and malleability—thinking that any environment that can be shaped is unpredictable—and thus divide the world of strategic possibilities into only two parts (predictable and immutable or unpredictable and mutable), whereas they ought to consider all four. So it did not surprise us to find that companies that match their strategic style to their environment perform significantly better than those that don't. In our analysis, the three-year total shareholder returns of companies in our survey that use the right style were 4% to 8% higher, on average, than the returns of those that do not.

Let's look at each style in turn.

Classical

When you operate in an industry whose environment is predictable but hard for your company to change, a classical strategic style has the best chance of success. This is the style familiar to most managers and business school graduates—five forces, blue ocean, and growth-share matrix analyses are all manifestations of it. A company sets a goal, targeting the most favorable market position it can attain by capitalizing on its particular capabilities

FIGURE 4-1

The right strategic style for your environment

Our research shows that approaches to strategy formulation fall into four buckets, according to how predictable an industry's environment is and how easily companies can change that environment.

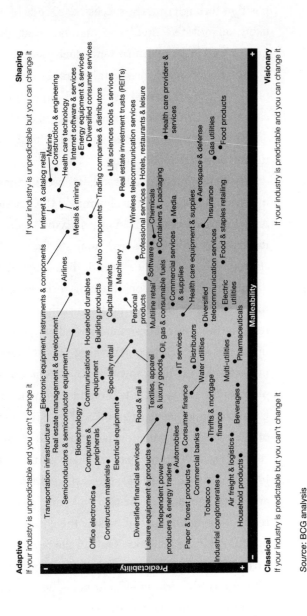

Adaptive
If your industry is unpredictable and you can't change it

Shaping
If your industry is unpredictable but you can change it

Classical
If your industry is predictable but you can't change it

Visionary
If your industry is predictable and you can change it

Source: BCG analysis

and resources, and then tries to build and fortify that position through orderly, successive rounds of planning, using quantitative predictive methods that allow it to project well into the future. Once such plans are set, they tend to stay in place for several years. Classical strategic planning can work well as a stand-alone function because it requires special analytic and quantitative skills, and things move slowly enough to allow for information to pass between departments.

Oil company strategists, like those in many other mature industries, effectively employ the classical style. At a major oil company such as ExxonMobil or Shell, for instance, highly trained analysts in the corporate strategic-planning office spend their days developing detailed perspectives on the long-term economic factors relating to demand and the technological factors relating to supply. These analyses allow them to devise upstream oil-extraction plans that may stretch 10 years into the future and downstream production-capacity plans up to five years out. It could hardly be otherwise, given the time needed to find and exploit new sources of oil, to build production facilities, and to keep them running at optimum capacity. These plans, in turn, inform multiyear financial forecasts, which determine annual targets that are focused on honing the efficiencies required to maintain and bolster the company's market position and performance. Only in the face of something extraordinary—an extended Gulf war; a series of major oil refinery shutdowns—would plans be seriously revisited more frequently than once a year.

Adaptive

The classical approach works for oil companies because their strategists operate in an environment in which the most attractive positions and the most rewarded capabilities today will, in all likelihood, remain the same tomorrow. But that has never been true for some industries, and, as has been noted before in *Harvard Business Review* ("Adaptability: The New Competitive Advantage," by Martin Reeves and Mike Deimler, HBR July–August 2011), it's becoming less and less true where global competition, technological innovation, social feedback loops, and economic uncertainty combine to make the environment radically and persistently unpredictable. In such an environment, a carefully crafted classical strategy may become obsolete within months or even weeks.

Companies in this situation need a more adaptive approach, whereby they can constantly refine goals and tactics and shift, acquire, or divest resources smoothly and promptly. In such a fast-moving, reactive environment, when predictions are likely to be wrong and long-term plans are essentially useless, the goal cannot be to optimize efficiency; rather, it must be to engineer flexibility. Accordingly, planning cycles may shrink to less than a year or even become continual. Plans take the form not of carefully specified blueprints but of rough hypotheses based on the best available data. In testing them out, strategy must be tightly linked with or embedded in operations, to best capture change signals and minimize information loss and time lags.

Specialty fashion retailing is a good example of this. Tastes change quickly. Brands become hot (or not) overnight. No amount of data or planning will grant fashion executives the luxury of knowing far in advance what to make. So their best bet is to set up their organizations to continually produce, roll out, and test a variety of products as quickly as they can, constantly adapting production in the light of new learning.

The Spanish retailer Zara uses the adaptive approach. Zara does not rely heavily on a formal planning process; rather, its strategic style is baked into its flexible supply chain. It maintains strong ties with its 1,400 external suppliers, which work closely with its designers and marketers. As a result, Zara can design, manufacture, and ship a garment to its stores in as little as two to three weeks, rather than the industry average of four to six months. This allows the company to experiment with a wide variety of looks and make small bets with small batches of potentially popular styles. If they prove a hit, Zara can ramp up production quickly. If they don't, not much is lost in markdowns. (On average, Zara marks down only 15% of its inventory, whereas the figure for competitors can be as high as 50%.) So it need not predict or make bets on which fashions will capture its customers' imaginations and wallets from month to month. Instead it can respond quickly to information from its retail stores, constantly experiment with various offerings, and smoothly adjust to events as they play out.

Zara's strategic style requires relationships among its planners, designers, manufacturers, and distributors that are entirely different from what a company like

ExxonMobil needs. Nevertheless, Exxon's strategists and Zara's designers have one critical thing in common: They take their competitive environment as a given and aim to carve out the best place they can within it.

Shaping

Some environments, as internet software vendors well know, can't be taken as given. For instance, in new or young high-growth industries where barriers to entry are low, innovation rates are high, demand is very hard to predict, and the relative positions of competitors are in flux, a company can often radically shift the course of industry development through some innovative move. A mature industry that's similarly fragmented and not dominated by a few powerful incumbents, or is stagnant and ripe for disruption, is also likely to be similarly malleable.

In such an environment, a company employing a classical or even an adaptive strategy to find the best possible market position runs the risk of selling itself short, being overrun by events, and missing opportunities to control its own fate. It would do better to employ a strategy in which the goal is to shape the unpredictable environment to its own advantage before someone else does—so that it benefits no matter how things play out.

Like an adaptive strategy, a shaping strategy embraces short or continual planning cycles. Flexibility is paramount, little reliance is placed on elaborate prediction mechanisms, and the strategy is most commonly implemented as a portfolio of experiments. But unlike adapters, shapers focus beyond the boundaries of their own company, often by rallying a formidable ecosystem of customers, suppliers, and/or complementors to their cause by defining attractive new markets, standards, technology platforms, and business practices. They propagate these through marketing, lobbying, and savvy partnerships. In the early stages of the digital revolution, internet software companies frequently used shaping strategies to create new communities, standards, and platforms that became the foundations for new markets and businesses.

That's essentially how Facebook overtook the incumbent MySpace in just a few years. One of Facebook's savviest strategic moves was to open its social-networking platform to outside developers in 2007, thus attracting all manner of applications to its site. Facebook couldn't hope to predict how big or successful any one of them would become. But it didn't need to. By 2008 it had attracted 33,000 applications; by 2010 that number had risen to more than 550,000. So as the industry developed and more than two-thirds of the successful social-networking apps turned out to be games, it was not surprising that the most popular ones—created by Zynga, Playdom, and Playfish—were operating from, and enriching, Facebook's site. What's more, even if the social-networking landscape shifts dramatically as time goes on, chances are the most popular applications will still be on Facebook. That's because by creating a flexible and popular platform, the company actively shaped the business environment to its own advantage rather than merely staking out a position in an existing market or reacting to changes, however quickly, after they'd occurred.

Visionary

Sometimes, not only does a company have the power to shape the future, but it's possible to know that future and to predict the path to realizing it. Those times call for bold strategies—the kind entrepreneurs use to create entirely new markets (as Edison did for electricity and Martine Rothblatt did for XM satellite radio), or corporate leaders use to revitalize a company with a wholly new vision—as Ratan Tata is trying to do with the ultra-affordable Nano automobile. These are the big bets, the build-it-and-they-will-come strategies.

Like a shaping strategist, the visionary considers the environment not as a given but as something that can be molded to advantage. Even so, the visionary style has more in common with a classical than with an adaptive approach. Because the goal is clear, strategists can take deliberate steps to reach it without having to keep many options open. It's more important for them to take the time and care they need to marshal resources, plan thoroughly, and implement correctly so that the vision doesn't fall victim to poor execution. Visionary strategists must have the courage to stay the course and the will to commit the necessary resources.

Back in 1994, for example, it became clear to UPS that the rise of internet commerce was going to be a bonanza for delivery companies, because the one thing online retailers would always need was a way to get their offerings out of cyberspace and onto their customers' doorsteps. This future may have been just as clear to the much younger and smaller FedEx, but UPS had the means—

and the will—to make the necessary investments. That year it set up a cross-functional committee drawn from IT, sales, marketing, and finance to map out its path to becoming what the company later called "the enablers of global e-commerce." The committee identified the ambitious initiatives that UPS would need to realize this vision, which involved investing some $1 billion a year to integrate its core package-tracking operations with those of web providers and make acquisitions to expand its global delivery capacity. By 2000 UPS's multibillion-dollar bet had paid off: The company had snapped up a whopping 60% of the e-commerce delivery market.

Avoiding the Traps

In our survey, fully three out of four executives understood that they needed to employ different strategic styles in different circumstances. Yet judging by the practices they actually adopted, we estimate that the same percentage were using only the two strategic styles—classic and visionary—suited to predictable environments (see the sidebar "Which Strategic Style Is Used the Most?"). That means only one in four was prepared in practice to adapt to unforeseeable events or to seize an opportunity to shape an industry to his or her company's advantage. Given our analysis of how unpredictable their business environments actually are, this number is far too low. Understanding how different the various approaches are and in which environment each best applies can go a long way toward correcting mismatches between strategic style and business environment. But as strategists

WHICH STRATEGIC STYLE IS USED THE MOST?

Our survey found that companies were most often using the two styles best suited to predictable environments—classical and visionary—even when their environments were clearly unpredictable.

9%
Shaping

16%
Adaptive

35%
Classical

40%
Visionary

think through the implications of the framework, they need to avoid three traps we have frequently observed.

Misplaced confidence

You can't choose the right strategic style unless you accurately judge how predictable and malleable your environment is. But when we compared executives' perceptions with objective measures of their actual environments, we saw a strong tendency to overestimate both factors. Nearly half the executives believed they could control uncertainty in the business environment through their own actions. More than 80% said that achieving goals depended on their own actions more than on things they could not control.

Unexamined habits

Many executives recognized the importance of building the adaptive capabilities required to address unpredictable environments, but fewer than one in five felt sufficiently competent in them. In part that's because many executives learned only the classical style, through experience or at business school. Accordingly, we weren't surprised to find that nearly 80% said that in practice they begin their strategic planning by articulating a goal and then analyzing how best to get there. What's more, some 70% said that in practice they value accuracy over speed of decisions, even when they are well aware that their environment is fast-moving and unpredictable. As a result, a lot of time is being wasted making untenable predictions when a faster, more iterative, and more experimental approach would be more effective. Executives are also closely attuned to quarterly and annual financial reporting, which heavily influences their strategic-planning cycles. Nearly 90% said they develop strategic plans on an annual basis, regardless of the actual pace of change in their business environments—or even what they perceive it to be.

Culture mismatches

Although many executives recognize the importance of adaptive capabilities, it can be highly countercultural to implement them. Classical strategies aimed at achieving economies of scale and scope often create company cultures that prize efficiency and the elimination of variation. These can of course undermine the opportunity to experiment and learn, which is essential for an adaptive strategy. And failure is a natural outcome of experimentation, so adaptive and shaping strategies fare poorly in cultures that punish it.

Avoiding some of these traps can be straightforward once the differing requirements of the four strategic styles are understood. Simply being aware that adaptive planning horizons don't necessarily correlate well with the rhythms of financial markets, for instance, might go a long way toward eliminating ingrained planning habits. Similarly, understanding that the point of shaping and visionary strategies is to change the game rather than to optimize your position in the market may be all that's needed to avoid starting with the wrong approach.

Being more thoughtful about metrics is also helpful. Although companies put a great deal of energy into making predictions year after year, it's surprising how rarely they check to see if the predictions they made in the prior year actually panned out. We suggest regularly reviewing the accuracy of your forecasts and also objectively gauging predictability by tracking how often and to what extent companies in your industry change relative position in terms of revenue, profitability, and other performance measures. To get a better sense of the extent to which industry players can change their environment, we recommend measuring industry youthfulness, concentration, growth rate, innovation rate, and rate of technology change—all of which increase malleability.

Operating in Many Modes

Matching your company's strategic style to the predictability and malleability of your industry will align overall strategy with the broad economic conditions in which the company operates. But various company units may well operate in differing subsidiary or geographic markets that are more or less predictable and malleable than the industry at large. Strategists in these units and markets can use the same process to select the most effective style for their particular circumstances, asking themselves the same initial questions: How predictable is the environment in which our unit operates? How much power do we have to change that environment? The answers may vary widely. We estimate, for example, that the Chinese business environment overall has been almost twice as malleable and unpredictable as that in the United States, making shaping strategies often more appropriate in China.

Similarly, the functions within your company are likely to operate in environments that call for differing approaches to departmental planning. It's easy to imagine, for instance, that within the auto industry a classical style would work well for optimizing production but would be inappropriate for the digital marketing department, which probably has a far greater power to shape its environment (after all, that's what advertising aims to do) and would hardly benefit from mapping out its campaigns years in advance.

If units or functions within your company would benefit from operating in a strategic style other than the one best suited to your industry as a whole, it follows that you will very likely need to manage more than one strategic style at a time. Executives in our survey are well aware of this: In fact, fully 90% aspired to improve their ability to manage multiple styles simultaneously. The simplest but also the least flexible way to do this is to structure and run functions, regions, or business units that require differing strategic styles separately. Allowing teams within units to select their own styles gives you more flexibility in diverse or fast-changing environments but is generally more challenging to realize.

Finally, a company moving into a different stage of its life cycle may well require a shift in strategic style. Environments for startups tend to be malleable, calling for visionary or shaping strategies. In a company's growth and maturity phases, when the environment is less malleable, adaptive or classical styles are often best. For companies in a declining phase, the environment becomes more malleable again, generating opportunities for disruption and rejuvenation through either a shaping or a visionary strategy.

Once you have correctly analyzed your environment, not only for the business as a whole but for each of your functions, divisions, and geographic markets, and you have identified which strategic styles should be used, corrected for your own biases, and taken steps to prime your company's culture so that the appropriate styles can successfully be applied, you will need to monitor your environment and be prepared to adjust as conditions change over time. Clearly that's no easy task. But we believe that companies that continually match their strategic styles to their situation will enjoy a tremendous advantage over those that don't.

––––––––––––

Martin Reeves is a senior partner and managing director in the Boston Consulting Group's San Francisco office and the chairman of the BCG Henderson Institute. He is the coauthor of *Your Strategy Needs a Strategy* (Harvard Business Review Press, 2015). Follow him on Twitter @MartinKReeves. **Claire Love** is a New York–based project leader at BCG's Strategy Institute. **Philipp Tillmanns** is a consultant at BCG in Hamburg and a PhD candidate at RWTH Aachen University, in Germany.

CHAPTER 5

The Different Approaches Firms Use to Set Strategy

by Kimberly Teti, Mu-Jeung Yang, Nicholas Bloom, Jan W. Rivkin, and Raffaella Sadun

What is your strategy? Most senior executives can confidently answer this question.

How has that strategy changed over time? This one usually gets a quick answer too.

How do you make decisions about changing that strategy? Now it gets much more difficult.

The fact is, many senior executives struggle to describe how they make strategic decisions. That's a serious

Adapted from content posted on hbr.org, April 10, 2017 (product #H03LAM).

problem, since the process for making strategic decisions can shape the strategy itself. Making a strategy without knowing your process is like sailing without a compass. You are setting yourself up for a long, stressful journey. Even worse, if you eventually reach your destination, you may not realize that you're in the right place.

To better understand how companies really make strategic choices, we recently interviewed 92 current CEOs, founders, and senior executives. We asked each to answer detailed questions about their approach to strategic decision making. Their replies revealed both striking variety and underlying patterns. Here, we offer a typology of four approaches. Our results can't say that any single approach to strategy is always best, but we do offer some evidence that one of the approaches is often flawed.

Four Approaches to Strategic Decision Making

Companies' processes differed from each other in two ways. The first was whether a firm uses a high or low level of process to make strategic decisions. That is, does it have recurring routines for discussing strategy, triggering strategic changes, and reviewing those changes? The second was the amount of input from other employees that the leader considers while making a strategic decision. This factor focuses on employee involvement in decision making, not simply attendance at meetings or postdecision communication. These two factors can exist in any pairing, and based on our interviews, firms populate all boxes, which gives us four distinct archetypes of strategic decision making.

FIGURE 5-1

Four approaches to strategic decision making

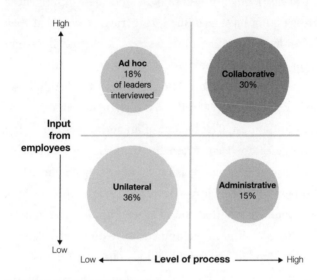

Note: Based on interviews with 92 executives

Unilateral firms are both low process and low input. They tend to have a top-down leader who makes decisions alone. During our interviews, these individuals often had difficulty explaining their decision-making process and the role other employees played. Interestingly, these interviewees had two different types of attitudes: Some disliked their process and admitted that they should do things differently, while others seemed very confident with how they made decisions. A potential benefit for unilateral firms is that leaders can make decisions quickly, without the constraints of process complexity and debate. However, lacking checks and balances, unilateral firms can make *bad* decisions fast. Moreover, speed is not a sure thing in a unilateral firm: If the top-down leader chooses to procrastinate on a tough decision, no process is in place to force timely action.

Ad hoc firms are low process and high input. These firms do not have a codified, recurring process that they follow every time they make a strategic change. But when a change needs to be made, the leader pulls their team together to take action. The exact steps the firm follows and the exact people in the room change from one decision to the next. The benefit of an ad hoc system is that rigid rules don't constrain the firm. Leaders can tailor the process to each decision by adjusting the length of deliberations, the involved parties, and other factors. The main risk is that the firm may not learn over time how to get better at making strategic decisions. The top leader of an ad hoc firm might also use the process flexibility to exclude stakeholders who disagree with the leader's position. This will eliminate the debate that fuels ad hoc decision making, and, in essence, shift the firm down to the unilateral box.

Administrative firms are high process but low input. These firms follow rigorous processes and well-defined routines to make strategic decisions without actually eliciting debate from other employees. One benefit is the detailed data collection and documentation that accompanies this extensive process. If administrative firms are smart, they can leverage this information to improve future decision making. But, similar to unilateral firms, the low level of input can result in bad decisions if leaders do not consider key information or opinions. In fact, this risk can be especially grave in administrative firms because the detailed process and the sheer quantity of information gathered can act as theater, masking the lack of broad input from internal and external stakeholders.

Collaborative firms are both high process and high input. These firms have the rigorous process of an administrative firm, but also the engaged employees of an ad hoc firm. During interviews, these leaders showed strong consistency across different types of decisions and could clearly articulate how employees added value during the process. The detailed process ensures that the leaders don't miss any steps. The frequent input ensures that they don't miss any information. However, the inflexible system can potentially slow down decision making and prevent firms from acting on time-sensitive opportunities. For example, collaborative firms may inadvertently include irrelevant parties in strategy discussions or spend too much time achieving consensus among the participants in order to maintain engagement.

Which Approach Should a Firm Use?

Each of these archetypes has benefits and risks, which invites a question: Where should a firm sit in the matrix? Our interview data shows tremendous variation in archetype within each industry and across firms of similar size, which suggests that the right archetype for a given firm depends on subtle features of the company and its context. Our current research does not include enough data on context and firm performance to pinpoint the conditions in which one archetype would be the winner.

That said, our early data does make us skeptical about the unilateral archetype. In our interviews, we asked managers to give us a sense of where their approach stood in terms of five attributes that are generally associated with good strategic decision-making processes, namely:

- **Alternatives.** Does the firm consider alternative options when making strategic decisions?

- **Information.** How much information does the firm use to spark debate about decisions?

- **Implementation.** Is a detailed implementation plan available when a decision is made?

- **Learning.** Does the firm study successes and failures to learn for future decisions?

- **Communication.** Does the firm have a clear plan to communicate changes to employees?

We then scored executives' responses based on a quantitative rubric. Figure 5-2 shows the percentage of total possible points that the average firm in each archetype scored on each of the attributes. Unilateral firms scored lower on all criteria, to the point of statistical significance, than collaborative firms; on four of the five than administrative firms; and on three of the five than ad hoc firms. The low scores of unilateral firms raise a red flag about this approach. If you are using the unilateral archetype, you should pressure-test it and consider whether it is the best option for your firm. In contrast, the other three archetypes do not differ much in terms of the five attributes. For example, the chances of establishing learning routines appear very similar across ad hoc, collaborative, and administrative archetypes.

FIGURE 5-2

How different strategic approaches compare

Based on five attributes associated with good decision making.

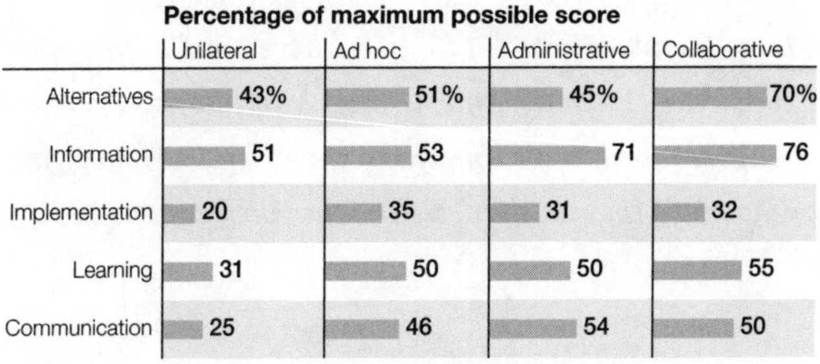

Percentage of maximum possible score

	Unilateral	Ad hoc	Administrative	Collaborative
Alternatives	43%	51%	45%	70%
Information	51	53	71	76
Implementation	20	35	31	32
Learning	31	50	50	55
Communication	25	46	54	50

Note: The closer to 100%, the more one's answers suggest decision making near the frontier. Based on interviews with 92 executives.

Ultimately, the wide variation in strategy-making approaches, even within similar industries and across organizations of similar sizes, was a real eye-opener for our research team. An optimistic interpretation of this finding is that managers have considerable leeway to choose the archetype that best fits their specific context. A less rosy interpretation is that managers may inadvertently be stuck with less-than-optimal approaches. Our future research will aim to shed more light on this important question.

In the meantime, our advice to leaders is to take a hard look at how they make strategic decisions. Where does your firm sit on the matrix? Does your approach match where you *want* to be, given the pros and cons of each archetype? Does the approach fit with the demands of your market and firm? Questions like these will show whether you need to change and will help you start the work needed to shift processes and culture to find a new home on the matrix.

The authors are grateful to Alek Duerksen, David Lopez-Lengowski, Michael Lynch, Meg McGuire, and Jackie Reilly, who conducted many of the interviews and gave insightful input on the design of the survey instrument.

Kimberly Teti was an MBA candidate at Harvard Business School at the time of this research and the original article's publication. She now works for Boston Consulting Group in Washington, DC. **Mu-Jeung Yang** is a visiting assistant professor of finance at the Eccles School of Business, University of Utah. Previously, he was an assistant professor of economics at the University of Washington. **Nicholas Bloom** is the William Eberle Professor of Economics at Stanford University and a codirector of the Productivity, Innovation and Entrepreneurship program at the National Bureau of Economic Research. **Jan W. Rivkin** is the Bruce V. Rauner Professor at Harvard Business School. **Raffaella Sadun** is the Thomas S. Murphy Associate Professor of Business Administration at Harvard Business School, where she studies the economics of productivity, organization, management practices, and information technology.

CHAPTER 6

Six Tips for Running Offsites That Aren't a Waste of Time

by Melissa Raffoni

Let's face it. Team strategy offsite meetings are expensive and time-consuming. While these events can provide a great environment for team building and alignment, such benefits can be short-lived and easily lost when team members move back into their day-to-day operations.

Adapted from content posted on hbr.org, July 22, 2019 (product #H0523M).

For the past 20 years, my team and I have worked closely with CEOs to plan and facilitate annual strategic planning offsites for executive teams. With facilitating these meetings comes the responsibility to drive sustained results. We've learned what it takes to make offsites "sticky"—meaning that the outcomes team members walk away with have an ongoing impact on their business.

Whether you are running a small executive team offsite or one for a larger group, here are six tips to make sure your next event has a lasting impact:

1. Be Crystal Clear About Your Objectives

Before the offsite, make sure you and your team identify what you hope to achieve during the event, as well as how you will measure success after it. Your objectives might include:

- Working together to develop a set of strategic priorities and desired measurable outcomes that the team fully commits to.

- Developing a plan for follow-through and accountability with respect to achieving these goals after the event.

- Facilitating a structured and thoughtful discussion on how the team can improve performance.

As you craft your objectives, consider the following questions: What do you want the participants to understand, agree to, rally around, and ultimately act on? How do you want them to feel after the meeting, and what can you do to drive that?

Sticky tip: Complete the following statement, "I'd be really happy if, by the end of our offsite, we [*fill in objectives here*]." This clarity will help you set expectations with your team when you discuss the objectives of the offsite beforehand. It will also strengthen their confidence and increase their engagement by allowing them to prepare for the discussion.

2. Think Twice About Who Should Be Invited

In our experience, leaders often make the mistake of inviting too many people to their offsites. When making your list of invitees, look closely at your objectives and ask yourself, "Am I better off with a large group or a handful of key people who can work closely to develop a strategy?" While having a larger group may be more inclusive, the productivity of your meeting has the potential to decrease.

Larger groups often require you to engage more people, which can result in a more superficial discussion. When people with varying levels of authority and skill sets are sitting around a table, there is a greater chance that politics, fear, or personal agendas will throw you off course. This can distract from the real conversations that need to happen for the event to meet your objectives. Inviting a smaller number of key people will allow you to have those conversations more easily.

Sticky tip: Map your attendee list to your objectives and make hard decisions about who to include if you must. It's usually best to invite the executive-level team first. Get them aligned. Then, once the core team is on the same page, designate some time at the offsite to figure out the best approach for engaging the next level of employees once you return to the office.

3. Develop a Detailed Agenda

Once you have a clear set of objectives and an invite list, it's time to create an agenda. Plan for each topic of discussion to last between 45 minutes to two hours maximum—this ensures that topics are neither cut too short nor watered down by having too much time allotted. With these guidelines in mind, you will likely be able to cover four to six topics in a full day. Your agenda planning should include:

- Topics of discussion (i.e., leader vision presentation, SWOT analysis, goal prioritization, team performance discussion)

- Specific objectives for each topic (i.e., understand leader direction, agree on SWOT, commit to three strategic goals, list three things the team can improve on)

- The types of activity or delivery modes you want to use (i.e., small group working sessions, large group facilitated discussions, brainstorms, knowledge presentations, panel discussions, Q&A sessions, games)

- The amount of time you want to designate to each topic

- A plan for the preparation work that needs to be done beforehand—by you, the organizer, or the team

Sticky tip: When you complete your agenda draft, check it against your objectives. You should be able to map each topic and activity back to each objective. Make sure everything lines up before finalizing. It may take a few rounds. You should also try to vary the delivery modes you decide upon. This will keep the energy of the team up and help participants stay engaged throughout the meeting.

4. Prepare the Logistics, Messaging, Materials, and Templates

While the basic logistics of transportation, food, sleeping arrangements, social events, and the meeting venue will need to be arranged by someone on the team, don't let this distract you from the more strategic task at hand— planning the higher-level details that will ensure stickiness. Take time well in advance of the event to work on the following:

- **Well-thought-out messaging.** How will you communicate objectives and expectations for the offsite, both prior and during? How will you frame the agenda? If you are assigning prework, how will you communicate the purpose and importance of it?

- **Quality and vetted communication materials.**
  What presentations or handouts are needed for
  the sessions you've mapped out? Who needs to
  be involved? What's the time line for completing
  them prior to the offsite?

- **Thoughtfully designed templates.** What documents need to be prepared in advance to help you
  capture the work being done at the event?

Sticky tips: Walk through the agenda to determine what
templates you need. Some examples might include a
SWOT grid, a KPI dashboard, a scorecard to capture
strategic goals and targeted measurable outcomes, or a
meetings/governance plan template.

We also recommend that you, as the leader of the offsite, create a thoughtful kickoff presentation to give at the
start of the offsite. Doing so will set your team up to dig
into the work. Plan for it to be about 45–75 minutes, depending on your objectives. Engage others to help you prepare your presentation or offer feedback in advance, and
try to anticipate or collect questions from the audience
beforehand. You should also be sure to include scheduled
time for a Q&A following the presentation. Think of it as
a way to align and set expectations with your team, both
with respect to the offsite and the business in general.

5. Focus on the Big Picture, Not Everyday Work

Well-planned offsites that see lasting results move above
the day-to-day operations and concentrate on the larger
picture. Think of this time as an opportunity to do just

that. Focus on strategic thinking and important issues that you haven't had time to think about at the office. Tune out mobile phones and leave laptops closed so you aren't pulled back into everyday tasks.

For example, you might use this time to make a decision you've been avoiding or haven't had the resources to tackle. It could be phasing out a product line that is not viable, addressing a low retention rate, improving cross-departmental collaboration, or a big idea, like expanding to other geos.

As you start to record team feedback, decisions, or goals, say no to flip charts, and instead, use an adapter to connect your computer to a larger screen and record notes live with your team. The visual will help them digest the information and allow you to have typed notes available for everyone immediately after the offsite. They will have the documents in their inboxes before they are back in the office and can start putting the agreed-upon plans to work right away.

Sticky tip: As you move through the offsite, reference this idea of "working *on* the business" to pull people out of the weeds as needed. Frequently ask: What problem are we trying to solve? At what level do we need to be addressing this? What do we need to do to make sure we follow through on this after we leave this meeting?

6. At the Close of the Event, Create a Team Governance Plan

To make sure the learnings and strategies you developed during the offsite are acted upon, take some time near the close of the event to discuss, as a team, what each person needs to do to drive the agreed-upon plan forward. Then, be sure to schedule enough progress check-ins to ensure success. Outside of high-quality output from your offsite, well-managed follow-up meetings are the single most important factor in ensuring stickiness.

As you develop your governance plan, ask:

- How will we hold each other accountable for executing the plans and decisions agreed to at the offsite?

- What needs to go on the calendar?

- For each required check-in, who needs to be there and what is the agenda?

- How often should these meetings occur, and how much time is needed to accomplish the goals on the agenda?

- Can the meetings be conducted virtually or do they need to be in-person?

For example, if one of your goals from the offsite is to improve the working relationship between sales and delivery, then you may need to schedule regular weekly meetings with those two departments aimed at making that happen.

Sticky tip: Agree on your governance plan at the offsite, and schedule your first few check-in meeting dates with the group while they are present. This will help everyone commit to follow-through, give you a forum to revisit the goals you established, and provide you with an opportunity to course correct if necessary. Don't be surprised if your team is resistant to more meetings. The key is to emphasize the importance of follow-through while being thoughtful about how many meetings need to happen, how long they need to be, and who should be involved. Seek to create a plan that drives results but does not waste people's time.

The combination of thoughtful planning prior to your offsite and mindful follow-through after will make this event "sticky" and well worth the investment. Your team will not only be more engaged, aligned, and prepared to better execute but also grateful for the time spent. And more importantly, the health and success of the business will be better for it.

———————

Melissa Raffoni is the founder and CEO of The Raffoni Group, a professional services firm that helps CEOs realize their highest ambitions while improving the quality of their personal and professional lives. She is recognized for her thought leadership and relevant experience in the areas of strategy development, leadership team alignment, organizational performance, and the role of the CEO.

CHAPTER 7

Stakeholders First, Strategy Second

by Graham Kenny

What stakeholders do you depend on for success?

When setting strategy, it might seem obvious that you'd need to ask this question. But most managers, even at the world's largest companies, don't think about it. Instead, they focus on a narrow set of key performance indicators and wade right into developing solutions that feed those metrics, burrowing deeper and deeper into the details. Very quickly they lose their "helicopter view" and get stuck in fix-it mode. Suggestions come one after

---

Adapted from "A List of Goals Is Not a Strategy" on hbr.org, November 19, 2014 (product #H01P99).

another: Engage sales outlets. Devise an advertising program. Attract, retain, and develop capable people. Good stuff, perhaps, but how would you know if you haven't defined a context for success?

Your organization or unit is completely dependent on others outside it for its good fortune. Without the support of stakeholders such as customers, suppliers, employees, and shareholders, for example, you *have* no organization. But you must identify those who are key to the long-term survival and prosperity of your organization—and then satisfy them.

Here, we should take a lesson from John Mackey, cofounder and co-CEO of Whole Foods Market. His company has annual sales of $9 billion and more than 300 stores. It dominates U.S. natural-foods retailing and has become an iconic brand. In a *Harvard Business Review* interview, Mackey describes what has brought success to Whole Foods. "Customers, employees, investors, suppliers, larger communities, and the environment are all interdependent," he explains. "Management's job at Whole Foods is to make sure that we hire good people, that they are well trained, and that they flourish in the workplace, because we found that when people are really happy in their jobs, they provide much higher degrees of service to the customers. Happy team members result in happy customers. Happy customers do more business with you. They become advocates for your enterprise, which results in happy investors. That is a win, win, win, win strategy."[1]

It's essential to think about who your stakeholders are *before* diving into strategy discussions. But simply identifying these groups or individuals is not enough. You must also think carefully about their wants and needs—as well as your own—to have a better understanding of how they align with your potential strategy.

Recognize What You Want from Your Stakeholders

When management teams begin to think about their key stakeholders, they often launch right into what they need to do *for* customers, *for* employees, and so on, without thinking first about what they want *from* them.

Why is sorting out the "from" so important? What an organization wants from each group of key stakeholders translates neatly into its objectives. For instance, sales and revenue growth will come from customers, productivity and innovation from employees, and quality goods and services at the right price from suppliers. What's more, company law requires that boards, CEOs, and senior executives act in the best interests of the *company*. All decision making should stem from that mandate. Of course, this doesn't preclude looking after customers' and other stakeholders' interests en route.

Although objectives and clear targets aren't a substitute for strategy, you do need to design them, stakeholder group by stakeholder group, before you can develop a smart strategy for each group. (See the sidebar "Creating a Value Proposition for Stakeholder Groups.") Otherwise, any old strategy will do. Unfortunately, strategies are often created in a vacuum. They won't be meaningful if you haven't decided what you want them to achieve.

CREATING A VALUE PROPOSITION FOR STAKEHOLDER GROUPS

by Jack Springman

It's helpful to create a value proposition for each stakeholder group you are targeting and detail how you will create value for that group. Typically there are three dimensions of value—financial (price, volume, margin, ROI, etc.), functional (increasing stakeholder's productivity, providing choice or flexibility, being easy and convenient to do business with, and delivering speedy service), and emotional (providing security to generate trust and stimulating a feel-good factor). All of these can be offered in some form to each group.

This value creation for each stakeholder group needs to be balanced by what the business will gain in return—the value it will extract from the relationship. Determine what you are seeking from each stakeholder group, both financially and operationally (in terms of loyalty, referrals, prioritization, etc.).

Knowing what value you want to offer, and what you hope to get in return, will allow you to identify what stakeholder-facing capabilities you need in order to execute. Compare the capabilities you need with those that you already have to highlight any gaps. You'll have to fill those gaps in through organizational redesign, training, process development, systems implementation, and cultural change.

Track the costs and benefits associated with each value proposition, including the investment necessary to complete the initiatives required to fill the capability gaps you've identified. Use this information to create a profit model to manage the inevitable trade-offs among your stakeholder groups. You may not be able to afford all the things you would like to do, but the profit model becomes the means for managing competing interests and the returns provided to each stakeholder group— the output being your financial returns (which are central to the value proposition to shareholders).

Finally, you need to determine a set of key performance indicators. These should track how effectively your business is creating value for each stakeholder group and how well you're capturing value in return. This will enable you to develop a stakeholder scorecard that provides a 360-degree view of performance.

Defining the value created for and from each stakeholder group adds perspective, ensuring that you look at your business from all angles. And by focusing on value creation for all your different stakeholders, you will be a creating a business that is more sustainable— in all senses of the word.

———

Jack Springman is a consultant specializing in growth strategies and the author of *Elusive Growth: Why Prevailing Practices in Strategy, Marketing, and Management Education Are the Problem, Not the Solution*.

Adapted from "Implementing a Stakeholder Strategy" on hbr.org, July 28, 2011.

Recognize What Your Stakeholders Want from You

When management teams delve too quickly into problem solving, they make assumptions. They think they already know what's good for their stakeholders. As a result, their companies end up with products and services that don't sell.

When you articulate what key stakeholders want, you're defining what I call "strategic factors." (They're not the same as "critical success factors"—a term you might already use. Those are generated by your management team, whereas strategic factors come from your stakeholders.) Strategic factors bring an external perspective. They are those *few* things that you must excel at if you are to achieve a competitive advantage and, simultaneously, meet your corporate objectives.

Here's a list of strategic factors from a company that manages a port and aims to attract as many ship operators as possible:

- Port capability (suitability for a ship's size and freight)

- Freight availability (to pick up on the return leg)

- Congestion (speed of unloading and turnaround time in the port)

- Location (which affects "steaming time," or time between destinations)

- Price (port charges for docking and remaining moored)

Note how these are defined from a stakeholder's point of view, not from management's. If you're not sure of them (that's the norm), interview your stakeholders to better understand their stories and needs.

Before diving into strategy and writing your strategic plan, thoughtfully consider who your strategy serves— and what you'd like from these individuals in return. By identifying your stakeholders, you can define a clearer strategy and objectives for your organization, so you can get the buy-in and support your plans deserve.

Graham Kenny, CEO of Strategic Factors, is a recognized expert in strategy. He is passionate about helping managers, executives, and boards create successful organizations in the private, public, and not-for-profit sectors. He does this through seminars and workshops on strategy and performance measurement; through keynote speaking; by working with managers to develop their business strategy and performance scorecards; and by publishing books, articles, and manuals. You can connect to or follow him on LinkedIn.

NOTE

1. Justin Fox, "What Is It That Only I Can Do?" *Harvard Business Review*, January–February 2011 (product #R1101J).

Develop Your Strategy

CHAPTER 8

Strategy Needs Creativity

by Adam Brandenburger

I've noticed that business school students often feel frustrated when they're taught strategy. There's a gap between what they learn and what they'd like to learn. Strategy professors (including me) typically teach students to think about strategy problems by introducing them to rigorous analytical tools—assessing the five forces, drawing a value net, plotting competitive positions. The students know that the tools are essential, and they dutifully learn how to use them. But they also realize that the tools are better suited to understanding an existing business context than to dreaming up ways

Reprinted from *Harvard Business Review*, March–April 2019 (product #R1902C).

to reshape it. Game-changing strategies, they know, are born of creative thinking: a spark of intuition, a connection between different ways of thinking, a leap into the unexpected.

They're right to feel this way—which is not to say that we should abandon the many powerful analytical tools we've developed over the years. We'll always need them to understand competitive landscapes and to assess how companies can best deploy their resources and competencies there. But we who devote our professional lives to thinking about strategy need to acknowledge that just giving people those tools will not help them break with conventional ways of thinking. If we want to teach students—and executives—how to generate groundbreaking strategies, we must give them tools explicitly designed to foster creativity.

A number of such tools already exist, often in practitioner-friendly forms. In "How Strategists Really Think: Tapping the Power of Analogy" (HBR, April 2005), Giovanni Gavetti and Jan W. Rivkin write compellingly about using analogies to come up with new business models. Charles Duhigg talks in his book *Smarter Faster Better* about introducing carefully chosen creative "disturbances" into work processes to spur new thinking. Youngme Moon, in "Break Free from the Product Life Cycle" (HBR, May 2005), suggests redefining products by boldly limiting—rather than augmenting—the features offered.

What these approaches have in common is the goal of moving strategy past the insights delivered by analytic tools (which are close at hand) and into territory that's further afield, or—to use a bit of academic jargon—*cognitively distant.* They take their inspiration more from how our thought processes work than from how industries or business models are structured. For that reason they can help strategists make the creative leap beyond what already exists to invent a genuinely new way of doing business. Simply waiting for inspiration to strike is not the answer.

In this article I explore four approaches to building a breakthrough strategy: (1) *Contrast.* The strategist should identify—and challenge—the assumptions undergirding the company's or the industry's status quo. This is the most direct and often the most powerful way to reinvent a business. (2) *Combination.* Steve Jobs famously said that creativity is "just connecting things"; many smart business moves come from linking products or services that seem independent from or even in tension with one another. (3) *Constraint.* A good strategist looks at an organization's limitations and considers how they might actually become strengths. (4) *Context.* If you reflect on how a problem similar to yours was solved in an entirely different context, surprising insights may emerge. (I wrote about these ideas more academically in "Where Do Great Strategies Really Come From?" *Strategy Science,* December 2017.) These approaches aren't exhaustive—or even entirely distinct from one another—but I've found that they help people explore a wide range of possibilities.

Contrast

What pieces of conventional wisdom are ripe for contradiction?

To create a strategy built on contrast, first identify the assumptions implicit in existing strategies. Elon Musk seems to have a knack for this approach. He and the other creators of PayPal took a widely held but untested assumption about banking—that transferring money online was feasible and safe between institutions but not between individuals—and disproved it. With SpaceX he is attempting to overturn major assumptions about space travel: that it must occur on a fixed schedule, be paid for by the public, and use onetime rockets. He may be on track toward a privately funded, on-demand business that reuses rockets.

It's best to be precise—even literal—when naming such assumptions. Consider the video rental industry in 2000. Blockbuster ruled the industry, and the assumptions beneath its model seemed self-evident: People pick up videos at a retail location close to home. Inventory must be limited because new videos are expensive. Since the demand for them is high, customers must be charged for late returns. (It was basically a public-library model.) But Netflix put those assumptions under a microscope. Why is a physical location necessary? Mailing out videos would be cheaper and more convenient. Is there a way around the high fees for new releases? If the studios were open to a revenue-sharing agreement, both parties could benefit. Those two changes allowed Netflix to carry lots more movies, offer long rental periods, do away with late fees—and remake an industry.

Most of the time, strategy from contrast may look less revolutionary than Netflix (which remade itself again by streaming videos and becoming a content creator) or SpaceX (should it succeed). Any organization can ask whether it might usefully flip the order in which it performs activities, for example. The traditional model in retail is to start with a flagship store (usually in a city center) and add satellites (in suburban locations). Now consider pop-up stores: In some cases they conform to the old model—they are like mini-satellites; but in others the pop-up comes first, and if that's successful, a larger footprint is added. The Soho area of New York City has become a testing ground for this strategy.

Another approach is to consider shaking up the value chain, which in any industry is conventionally oriented in a particular way, with some players acting as suppliers and others as customers. Inverting the value chain may yield new business models. In the charitable sector, for example, donors have been seen as suppliers of financial resources. DonorsChoose.org is a model that treats them more like customers. The organization puts up a "storefront" of requests posted by schoolteachers around the United States who are looking for materials for their (often underresourced) classrooms. Donors can choose which requests to respond to and receive photos of the schoolwork that their money has supported. In effect, they are buying the satisfaction of seeing a particular classroom before and after.

In some industries the status quo has dictated highly bundled, expensive products or services. Unbundling them is another way to build a contrast strategy. Various segments of the market may prefer to get differing subsets of the bundle at better prices. Challengers' un-bundling of the status quo has been facilitated by the internet in one industry after another: Music, TV, and education are leading examples. Incumbents have to make major internal changes to compete with unbun-dlers, rendering this approach especially effective.

How to begin

- Precisely identify the assumptions that under-lie conventional thinking in your company or industry.

- Think about what might be gained by proving one or more of them false.

- Deliberately disturb an aspect of your normal work pattern to break up ingrained assumptions.

What to watch out for

Because the assumptions underlying your business model are embedded in all your processes—and because stable businesses need predictability—it won't be easy to change course. Organizations are very good at resist-ing change.

Combination

How can you connect products or services that have traditionally been separate?

Combination is a canonical creative approach in both the arts and the sciences. As Anthony Brandt and David

Eagleman note in *The Runaway Species*, it was by combining two very different ideas—a ride in an elevator and a journey into space—that Albert Einstein found his way to the theory of general relativity. In business, too, creative and successful moves can result from combining things that have been separate. Often these opportunities arise with complementary products and services. Products and payment systems, for example, have traditionally been separate nodes in value chains. But the Chinese social media platform WeChat (owned by Tencent) now includes an integrated mobile payment platform called WeChat Pay that enables users to buy and sell products within their social networks. Expanding beyond the Chinese ecosystem, Tencent and Alibaba are coordinating with overseas payment firms to enable retailers in other countries to accept their mobile payment services.

Sometimes competitors can benefit from joining forces to grow the pie. (Barry Nalebuff and I explored this idea in our 1996 book *Co-opetition.*) For example, BMW and Daimler have announced plans to combine their mobility services—car sharing, ride hailing, car parking, electric vehicle charging, and tickets for public transport. Presumably, the two automakers hope that this move will be an effective counterattack against Uber and other players that are encroaching on the traditional car industry.

In other instances, companies from wholly separate industries have created new value for customers by combining offerings. Apple and Nike have done so since the 2006 introduction of the Nike+ iPod Sport Kit, which enabled Nike shoes to communicate with an iPod for tracking steps. More recently, versions of the Apple Watch have come with the Nike+ Run Club app fully integrated. Nest Labs and Amazon also complement each other: Nest's intelligent home thermostat becomes even more valuable when it can deploy voice control via Amazon's virtual assistant, Alexa.

New technologies are a rich source of combinatorial possibilities. AI and blockchain come together naturally to protect the privacy of the large amounts of personal data needed to train algorithms in health care and other sensitive areas. Blockchain and the internet of things come together in the form of sensors and secure data in decentralized applications such as food supply chains, transportation systems, and smart homes, with automated insurance included in smart contracts.

Perhaps the biggest combination today is the one emerging between humans and machines. Some commentators see the future of that relationship as more competitive than cooperative, with humans losing out in many areas of economic life. Others predict a more positive picture, in which machines take on lower-level cognition, freeing humans to be more creative. Martin Reeves and Daichi Ueda have written about algorithms that allow companies to make frequent, calibrated adjustments to their business models, enabling humans to work on high-level objectives and think beyond the present. (See "Designing the Machines That Will Design Strategy," hbr.org, April 2016.)

Strategy from combination involves looking for connections across traditional boundaries, whether by linking a product and a service, two technologies, the upstream and the downstream, or other ingredients. Here, too, the creative strategist must challenge the status quo—this time by thinking not just outside the box but across two or more boxes.

How to begin

- Form groups with diverse expertise and experience; brainstorm new combinations of products and services.

- Look for ways to coordinate with providers of complementary products (who may even be competitors).

What to watch out for

Businesses often manage for and measure profits at the individual product or activity level. But combinations require system-level thinking and measurements.

Constraint

How can you turn limitations or liabilities into opportunities?

The world's first science fiction story, *Frankenstein*, was written when its author, Mary Wollstonecraft Shelley, was staying near Lake Geneva during an unusually cold and stormy summer and found herself trapped indoors with nothing to do but exercise her imagination. Artists know a lot about constraints—from profound ones, such as serious setbacks in their lives, to structural ones, such as writing a 14-line poem with a specified rhyming structure. In business, too, creative thinking turns limitations into opportunities.

That constraints can spark creative strategies may seem paradoxical. Lift a constraint, and any action that was previously possible is surely still possible; most likely, more is now possible. But that misses the point that one can think multiple ways in a given situation—and a constraint may prompt a whole new line of thinking. Of course, the Goldilocks principle applies: Too many constraints will choke off all possibilities, and a complete absence of constraints is a problem too.

Tesla hasn't lacked financial resources in entering the car industry, but it doesn't have a traditional dealership network (considered a key part of automakers' business models) through which to sell. Rather than get into the business of building one, Tesla has chosen to sell cars online and to build Apple-like stores staffed with salespeople on salary. This actually positions the company well relative to competitors, whose dealers may be conflicted about promoting electric vehicles over internal-combustion ones. In addition, Tesla controls its pricing directly, whereas consumers who buy electric vehicles from traditional dealers may encounter significant variations in price.

I should note that this attitude toward constraints is very different from that suggested by the classic SWOT analysis. Strategists are supposed to identify the strengths, weaknesses, opportunities, and threats impinging on an organization and then figure out ways to exploit strengths and opportunities and mitigate weaknesses and threats.

In stark contrast, a constraint-based search would look at how those weaknesses could be turned to the company's advantage. Constraint plus imagination may yield an opportunity.

This approach to strategy turns the SWOT tool upside down in another way as well. Just as an apparent weakness can be turned into a strength, an apparent strength can prove to be a weakness. The likelihood of this often increases over time, as the assets that originally enabled a business to succeed become liabilities when the environment changes. For example, big retailers have historically considered "success" to be moving product out the door; to that end, they needed large physical footprints with on-site inventory. Among the many changes they face today is the rise of "guideshops"—a term used by the menswear retailer Bonobos—where shoppers try on items, which they can have shipped to them or later order online. In the new environment, traditional retail footprints become more of a liability than an asset.

Another way to approach strategy from constraint is to ask whether you might benefit from self-imposed constraints. (Artists do something similar when they choose to work only within a particular medium.) The famous Copenhagen restaurant Noma adheres to the New Nordic Food manifesto (emphasizing purity, simplicity, beauty, seasonality, local tradition, and innovation). A similar strategy of working only with local suppliers has been adopted by thousands of restaurants around the world. A commitment to high environmental standards, fair labor practices, and ethical supply-chain management can be powerful for organizations looking to lead change in their industries or sectors.

Self-imposed constraints can also spur innovation. Adam Morgan and Mark Barden, in their book *A Beautiful Constraint*, describe the efforts of the Audi racing team in the early 2000s to win Le Mans under the assumption that its cars couldn't go faster than the competition's. Audi developed diesel-powered racers, which required fewer fuel stops than gasoline-powered cars, and won Le Mans three years in succession (2004–2006). In 2017 Audi set itself a new constraint—and a new ambition: to build winning all-electric racers for the new Formula E championship.

How to begin

- List the "incompetencies" (rather than the competencies) of your organization—and test whether they can in fact be turned into strengths.

- Consider deliberately imposing some constraints to encourage people to find new ways of thinking and acting.

What to watch out for

Successful businesses face few obvious constraints; people may feel no need to explore how new ones might create new opportunities.

Context

*How can far-flung industries, ideas,
or disciplines shed light on your most
pressing problems?*

An entire field, biomimetics, is devoted to finding solutions in nature to problems that arise in engineering, materials science, medicine, and elsewhere. For example, the burrs from the burdock plant, which propagate by attaching to the fur of animals via tiny hooks, inspired George de Mestral in the 1940s to create a clothing fastener that does not jam (as zippers are prone to do). Thus the invention of Velcro. This is a classic problem-solving technique. Start with a problem in one context, find another context in which an analogous problem has already been solved, and import the solution.

Intel did that when it came up with its famous Intel Inside logo, in the early 1990s. The goal was to turn Intel microprocessors into a branded product to speed up consumers' adoption of next-generation chips and, more broadly, to improve the company's ability to drive the PC industry forward. Branded ingredients were well established in certain consumer product sectors—examples include Teflon and NutraSweet—but hadn't been tried in the world of technology. Intel imported the approach to high tech with a novel advertising campaign, successfully branding what had previously been an invisible computer component.

Context switching can be done across industries, as in Intel's case, or even across time. The development of the graphical user interface (GUI) for computers was in a sense the result of a step backward: The developers moved from immersion in the text-based context in which programming had grown up to thinking about the highly visual hand-eye environment in which young children operate. Similarly, some AI researchers are currently looking at how children learn in order to inform processes for machine learning.

Companies are always eager to see into the future, of course, and techniques for trying to do so are well established. That is the purpose of lead-user and extreme-user innovation strategies, which ask companies to shift their attention from mainstream customers to people who are designing their own versions or using products in unexpected ways in especially demanding environments. Information about where the edges of the market are today can signal where the mainstream will be tomorrow. Extreme sports, such as mountain biking, skateboarding, snowboarding, and windsurfing, are good examples. In an MIT Sloan School working paper, Sonali Shah relates that aficionados led many of the innovations in those areas, starting in the 1950s, and big manufacturers added cost efficiencies and marketing to take them mainstream.

When companies locate R&D functions far from headquarters, they're acknowledging the importance of jumping into someone else's context. This is not just a strategy for large companies that move people to Silicon Valley for tech or the Boston area for biotech. Startups, too, should put themselves in the best context for learning and growth. The hardware accelerator HAX, located in Shenzhen, hosts hardware startup teams from numerous countries and enables them to tap into the high-speed ecosystem of the "hardware capital of the world," quadrupling the rate at which they cycle through iterations of their prototypes.

Strategy focused on context may involve transferring a solution from one setting to another more or less as is. It may mean uncovering entirely new thinking about problems (or opportunities) by finding pioneers who are ahead of the game. At bottom, it's about not being trapped in a single narrative.

How to begin

- Explain your business to an outsider in another industry. Fresh eyes from a different context can help uncover new answers and opportunities.

- Engage with lead users, extreme users, and innovation hotspots.

What to watch out for

Businesses need to focus on internal processes to deliver on their current value propositions—but the pressure to focus internally can get in the way of learning from the different contexts in which other players operate.

Conclusion

In the world of management consulting, aspects of "strategy" and "innovation" have started to converge. IDEO, the design and innovation powerhouse, has moved into strategy consulting, for example—while

McKinsey has added design-thinking methods to its strategy consulting. This convergence raises an obvious question: If the distinction between strategy and innovation is less clear than it once was, do we really need to think carefully about the role of creativity in the strategy-making process?

I believe strongly that the answer is yes. At its core, strategy is still about finding ways to create and claim value through differentiation. That's a complicated, difficult job. To be sure, it requires tools that can help identify surprising, creative breaks from conventional thinking. But it also requires tools for analyzing the competitive landscape, the dynamics threatening that landscape, and a company's resources and competencies. We need to teach business school students—and executives—how to be creative and rigorous at the same time.

Adam Brandenburger holds positions as the J.P. Valles Professor at the Stern School of Business, Distinguished Professor at the Tandon School of Engineering, and faculty director of the Program on Creativity and Innovation at NYU Shanghai, all at New York University.

CHAPTER 9

Five Questions to Build a Strategy

by Roger L. Martin

People make strategy much harder than it needs to be. For some, the problem is that they focus too much on the tools: environmental scans, SWOT analyses, customer analyses, competitor analyses, financial modeling, and so on. Other people get into trouble because they think it's all about the broad, conceptual, future-oriented, big-picture stuff—not to be confused with tactics. Still other times, people think that strategy is what happens when we think about changing directions.

The reality is that strategy is at some level about all those things, and you can't do a satisfactory job with

Adapted from content posted on hbr.org, May 26, 2010 (product #H005PU) and "Strategic Choices Need to Be Made Simultaneously, Not Sequentially," on hbr.org, April 3, 2017 (product #H03K4Y).

your analysis alone, or your big picture alone, or your changes alone. You have to do a bit of work on all of them.

That's actually a lot easier than it sounds. My preferred approach is to treat strategy making as developing a set of answers to five interlinked questions. The questions—which cascade logically from the first to the last, as seen in figure 9-1—are as follows:

1. What are our broad **aspirations** for our organization and the concrete **goals** against which we can measure our progress?

2. Across the potential field available to us, **where will we choose to play** and not play?

3. In our chosen place to play, **how** will we choose **to win** against the competitors there?

4. What **capabilities** are necessary **to build** and maintain to win in our chosen manner?

5. What **management systems** are necessary **to operate** to build and maintain the key capabilities?

The trick is to have five answers that are consistent with one another and reinforce one another. "Aspirations and goals" to be a great international player and a "where to play" response that is domestic doesn't match well with a "how to win" on the basis of proprietary R&D—because the competitors with global aspirations will almost certainly out-invest and outflank you. Winning on the basis of superior distribution is unlikely to happen if you don't have a concrete plan to build the capabilities and a management system to maintain them.

FIGURE 9-1

The strategy choice cascade

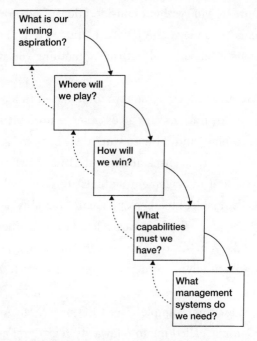

Source: A.G. Lafley and Roger L. Martin, *Playing to Win: How Strategy Really Works* (Boston: Harvard Business Review Press, 2013).

Moving Up and Down the Cascade

So where do you start? Most organizations start at the top with some kind of mission/vision exercise that drives participants around the bend. The reason it drives them crazy is that it is extremely difficult to create a meaningful aspiration/mission/vision in the absence of some idea of "where to play" and "how to win." That is why those conversations tend to go around in circles with nobody knowing how to actually agree on anything. Any mission or vision will do when you don't have a thought-through concept of "where to play" or "how to win."

That said, if you think entirely about "where to play" and "how to win" without consideration of "aspirations and goals," you may end up with a strategy that is effective for its intended goal but isn't something you would actually want.

To create a strategy, you have to iterate—think a little bit about "aspirations and goals," then a little bit about "where to play" and "how to win," then back to "aspirations and goals" to check and modify, then down to "capabilities and management systems" to check whether it is really doable, then back up again to modify accordingly. Each of the five boxes are related to each other. You must make your strategic choices simultaneously, rather than sequentially, in order for your strategy to make sense.

Consider this example. The CEO of a large Australian company called me to relay a strategy development problem his firm was facing and ask for my advice. My friend explained that each of his five business-unit presidents was using the strategy choice cascade, and that all of them had gotten stuck in the same place. They had chosen a "winning aspiration" and had settled on a "where to play" choice. But all of them were stuck at the "how to win" box.

It is no surprise, I told my friend, that they have gotten stuck. It is because they considered "where to play" without reference to "how to win."

The challenge here is that both are linked, and *together* they are the heart of strategy; without a great "where to play" and "how to win" combination, you can't possibly have a worthwhile strategy. Of course, "where to play" and "how to win" have to link with and reinforce an inspiring "winning aspiration." And "capabilities and management systems" act as a reality check on the "where to play" and "how to win" choices. If you can't identify a set of "capabilities and management systems" that you currently have, or can reasonably build, to make the "where to play" and "how to win" choices come to fruition, you have a fantasy, not a strategy.

Many people ask me why "capabilities and management systems" are part of strategy when they are really elements of execution. That is yet another manifestation of the widespread, artificial, and unhelpful attempt to distinguish between choices that are "strategic" and ones that are "executional" or "tactical." Remember that, regardless of what name you give them, these choices are a critical part of the integrated set of five choices that are necessary to successfully guide the actions of an organization.

I had to tell my Australian friend that locking and loading on "where to play" choices, rather than setting the table for a great discussion of "how to win," actually makes it virtually impossible to have a productive consideration of "how to win." That is because no meaningful "where to play" choice exists outside the context of a particular "how to win" plan. An infinite number of "where to play" choices are possible, and equally meritorious—before considering "how to win" for each. In other words, there aren't inherently strong and weak "where to play" choices. They are only strong or weak in the context of a particular "how to win" choice. Therefore, making lists of "where to play" choices before considering "how to win" choices has zero value in strategy.

Understanding Matched Pairs

You can find a number of relevant business examples that fell in the same trap my friend did. For example, Uber made a "where to play" choice that included China because it's a huge and important market. But being huge and important didn't make that choice inherently meritorious. It would have been meritorious only if there had been a clear "how to win" as well—which it appears there never was. Microsoft made a "where to play" choice to get into smartphone hardware (with its acquisition of Nokia's handset business) because it was a huge and growing market, seemingly adjacent to Microsoft's own, but it had no useful conception of how that would be twinned with a "how to win"—and it lost spectacularly. P&G made a "where to play" choice to get into the huge, profitable, and growing pharmaceutical business with the acquisition of Norwich Eaton in 1982. While it performed decently in the business, it divested the business in 2009 because, in those nearly two decades, it came to realize that it could play but never win in that still-exciting "where to play."

No meaningful "how to win" choice exists outside the context of a particular "where to play." Despite what many think, there are not generically great ways to win— for example, being a first mover or a fast follower or a branded player or a cost leader. All "how to win" choices are useful, or not, depending on the "where to play" with which they are paired. A "how to win" choice based on superior scale is not going to be useful if the "where to play" choice is to concentrate on a narrow niche—because that would undermine an attempted scale advantage.

Undoubtedly, Uber thought its "how to win"—having an easy-to-use ride-hailing app for users twinned with a vehicle for making extra money for drivers—would work well in any "where to play." But it didn't work in the "where to play" of China. It turned out that Uber's "how to win" had a lot to do with building a first-mover advantage in markets like the United States; when Uber was a late entrant, the "where to play" wasn't a simple extension, and it exited after losing convincingly to first mover Didi. Perhaps Microsoft felt that its "how to win" of having strong corporate relationships and a huge installed base of software users would extend nicely into smartphones, but it most assuredly didn't. As a Canadian, I can't help but recall the many Canadian retailers with powerful "how to wins" in Canada (Tim Hortons, Canadian Tire, Jean Coutu) that simply didn't translate to a "where to play" in the United States. Perhaps there is some solace, however, in retailer Target's disastrous attempt to extend its U.S. "how to win" into the Canadian "where to play"—turnabout is, I guess, fair play.

The only productive, intelligent way to generate possibilities for strategy choice is to consider *matched pairs* of "where to play" and "how to win" choices. Generate a variety of pairs and then ask about each:

- Can it be linked to an inspiring, attractive "winning aspiration"?

- Do we currently have, or can we reasonably build, the capabilities that would be necessary to win where we would play?

- Can we create the "management systems" that would need to be in place to support the building and maintenance of the necessary capabilities?

Those "where to play" and "how to win" possibilities for which these questions can plausibly be answered in the affirmative should be taken forward for more consideration and exploration. For the great success stories of our time, the tight match of "where to play" and "how to win" is immediately obvious. USAA sells insurance only to military personnel, veterans, and their families—and tailors its offerings brilliantly and tightly to the needs of those in that sphere, so much so that its customer satisfaction scores are off the charts. Vanguard sells index mutual funds/ETFs to customers who don't believe that active management is helpful to the performance of their investments. With that tight "where to play," it can win by working to achieve the lowest cost position in the business. Google wins by organizing the world's information, but to do that it has to play across the broadest swath of search.

While it may sound a bit daunting, iterating like this actually makes strategy easier. It will save you from endless visioning exercises, misdirected SWOT analyses, and lots of heroically uninformed big thinking. Crafting your strategy in relatively small and concrete chunks and honing the answers to the five questions through iteration will get you a better strategy, with much less pain and wasted time.

———————

Roger L. Martin is professor emeritus and former dean of the Rotman School of Management at the University of Toronto. He is a coauthor of *Creating Great Choices: A Leader's Guide to Integrative Thinking* (Harvard Business Review Press, 2017).

CHAPTER 10

Four Types of Competition That Can Threaten Your Company

by Carsten Lund Pedersen and Thomas Ritter

As uncertainty is increasing and competition is becoming more fierce, leaders and executives need to have a broader understanding of competition itself in order to sustain an edge. As a leader, you should be thinking about four different types of competition to maintain relevance in a changing environment, which originate from our work on competitiveness, strategy, and strategic change.

Adapted from "Stress Test Your Company's Competitive Edge with These 4 Questions" on hbr.org, June 5, 2018 (product #H04DBI).

FIGURE 10-1

The four types of competition

Use this 2x2 to identify which currently exposes you to the greatest challenge.

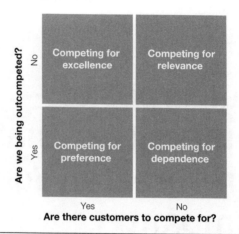

In figure 10-1, these four competition types are positioned along two dimensions, which reflect two distinct questions:

1. Are there customers for which to compete?

2. Are we being outcompeted?

These questions will help you identify the type of competition that currently exposes your organization to the greatest existential threats. Leaders who consider and discuss all four types of competition will uncover important insights, and such an analysis can help move your strategy forward.

The Four Types of Competition

Table 10-1 provides an overview of the four types of competition and the four key questions that help identify important strategic issues:

Competition for relevance

The first, and most fundamental, level of competition relates to competition for relevance. Here, executives must ask: "Does our offering meet and satisfy actual consumer needs?"

Technological developments are often interesting to discuss in relation to relevance. For instance, numerous

TABLE 10-1

Which types of competition threaten your company?

Ask yourself these questions regularly to help maintain a competitive edge.

Type of competition	Question	Competing for	Competing against	Example
Relevance	"Do our offerings satisfy real consumer needs?"	Consumer needs	Irrelevance	Blockchain
Dependence	"Can consumers supply their own solutions?"	Willingness to buy	Self-supply	The DIY economy
Preference	"Do customers prefer us to our competitors?"	Market share	Competitors	The retail industry
Excellence	"How can we renew our business?"	Renewal	Complacency	Nokia

smartphone apps have been developed that do not solve any actual problems. A current example of uncertainty around relevance concerns blockchain, the technology behind virtual currencies such as bitcoin. On one hand, there's the question of whether blockchain is essentially hype or whether it fulfills an actual need of the mainstream public. On the other hand, if the blockchain technology actually lives up to its promises of securing transparent and secure transmissions, then it will also challenge intermediaries such as brokers and bankers, who may no longer be needed. In other words, the technology can make brokers and bankers irrelevant. Consequently, the blockchain technology is a great example of the uncertainty that often accompanies new technological developments—they can either negate the relevance of established organizations or prove to be an unsustainable alternative without sufficient mainstream support.

Competition for dependence

When relevance is established, executives face another level of competition: competition for dependence. This refers to the notion that organizations also compete against consumers' abilities to satisfy their own needs and their jobs to be done. In other words, consumers can often create a solution for themselves, thereby making the organization's offering obsolete.

An example of the difficulties of competing for dependence can be seen in the rise of the "DIY-economy," which was particularly pronounced after the 2008 recession. At that time, many consumers adopted a new level of frugality, such that they took on previously outsourced tasks and became more self-reliant. For example, many consumers started to dye and cut their own hair, brew their own espressos, wash their own cars, clean their own houses, and walk their own dogs. This "in-sourcing" of household chores hurt many of the small, service-oriented businesses that had previously handled these tasks. However, some organizations have been able to capitalize on self-reliance. For instance, Target has run marketing campaigns that glorify do-it-yourself alternatives, while IKEA has become synonymous with enabling consumers to do the work themselves.

Competition for preference

Given relevance and dependence, the next battle is the competition for preference. Organizations compete to win customers' preference for their offerings over those of competitors.

An example of competition for preference can be seen in the retail industry, which has long been a battleground for customer preferences. Interestingly, customers have varied preferences for retailers depending on the product category. Therefore, the retail market is actually several markets. For example, customers may prefer Target for product category A, Walmart for product category B, Staples for product category C, and Amazon or Alibaba for product category D. Consequently, the battle with competitors for customer preference often takes place on the specific product-category level. Moreover, this form of competition can lead to price pressure, which may have a damaging effect on industry profits.

THE STATUS QUO IS RISKY, TOO

by Liane Davey

Armed only with the risks of changing, it's natural to shy away from decisive action. But failing to assess the risk of the status quo does not mean the risks won't materialize—it just means you won't be adequately prepared when they do. Here are several strategies you can employ to combat the risk of underestimating the status quo with your team.

- *Bring the discussion back to your current strategy.* Frame the conversation in terms of changes in what customers need or want. If the customers haven't changed much, point to changes in the competitive environment that make your strategy less sound today than it was when it was developed. Mine societal, economic, political, regulatory, and technological trends to identify any external changes that necessitate a shift in your strategy.

- *Develop a risk profile for your current strategy using the same framework you're using to assess your new strategic options.* If you have assessed the risk of your strategic options in terms of brand risk, operational risk, market risk, and so on, do the same for the current strategy. Focus the team on the incremental risk of the new options and highlight any places where the proposed strategy is actually less risky than the existing one.

- *Put boundaries in place.* If executives on your team are endlessly asking for more information, ask questions like, "How much do we need to know before we can make a good decision here?"

or "What would it take for you to have 80% confidence in this path?" or "What is our window for making this decision?" By calling attention to the indecisiveness and helping your teammates get more comfortable with acting in the absence of complete information, you are more likely to get traction to move beyond the status quo.

- **Deal with team dynamics that stem from turf issues or self-interest.** If you're seeing protectionist behavior on your team, invoke the best interests of the organization. For instance, I use the curves laid out in Clayton Christensen's *The Innovator's Dilemma* to show how continued incremental progress will leave the organization vulnerable to competitors. Then you can say something like, "What are we doing about the coming war over wearable computing? It's not here yet, but how do we ensure we're not irrelevant when wearables really gain momentum?"

We are more likely to evaluate the risk of changing than to evaluate the risk of staying the same. If your teammates are anchoring your business in the past, it's your responsibility to help them see the risk of the status quo.

———

Liane Davey is a team effectiveness adviser and professional speaker. She is the author of *The Good Fight* and *You First*, and the coauthor of *Leadership Solutions*. Follow her on Twitter @LianeDavey.

Adapted from content posted on hbr.org, May 2, 2014 (product #H00SI2).

However, the battle for customer preference is not solely fought in specific product and price categories—it is also fought in the domains of location and promotional expenditure.

Competition for excellence

After successfully competing for relevance, dependence, and preference, organizations must consider competition for excellence. At this level, the challenge is to sustain the organization's advantage while continuously seeking renewal.

An example of a failure to compete for excellence is illustrated by how Nokia, in the midst of its success, failed to keep up with the competitive threats from Apple. Despite being a leader in the mobile phone market with a market share of over 40%, Nokia experienced a dramatic decline that led to a sale of its mobile phone business to Microsoft in 2013. The demise was partly caused by a competitive shift toward software and ecosystems rather than hardware; Nokia did not appropriately adapt to this environment due to conservatism and a belief in its existing strengths. Put differently, Nokia's past success acted as a blinder to peripheral threats coming from unexpected sides. (For tips on how to respond to those who resist change, see the sidebar "The Status Quo Is Risky, Too.")

How to Use the Four Questions

How can executives actively ask these four questions and compete on all four levels to ensure renewal and sustain corporate performance? Executives can introduce three initiatives:

- **Put the questions on the agenda and regularly challenge your strategy:** The four types of competition should be used as a checklist for regularly challenging the strategy. Asking questions about the strategic plan is necessary for stress-testing a strategy (a topic discussed in more detail in chapter 14) and for applying a moderate amount of stress to your strategy.

- **Let different employee types discuss the four questions:** It can be beneficial to invite different types of employees to discuss the four questions, including employees at different hierarchical levels and different types of project managers.

- **Implement strategic projects for all four types:** The four types of competition can provide a categorization tool for different types of projects with which an organization can compete. For instance, companies can have a project where they collaborate with users to develop or refine a specific product or feature. Such an approach would improve the "competing for relevance" and "competing for dependence" dimensions, as it would secure user relevance while proactively codeveloping user dependence.

Competition is a multifaceted concept that plays out in different ways. Therefore, leaders and executives need to keep their eyes on all four types of competition in order to keep up with an ever-changing world.

Carsten Lund Pedersen is an assistant professor at the Department of Marketing at Copenhagen Business School, where he researches B2B digitization, market strategies, and frontline autonomy. **Thomas Ritter** is a professor of market strategy and business development at the Department of Strategy and Innovation at Copenhagen Business School, where he researches business model innovation, market strategies, and market management.

CHAPTER 11

How to Do Strategic Planning Like a Futurist

by Amy Webb

I recently helped a large industrial manufacturing company with its strategic planning process. With so much uncertainty surrounding autonomous vehicles, 5G, robotics, global trade, and the oil markets, the company's senior leaders needed a set of guiding objectives and strategies linking the company's future to the present day. Before our work began in earnest, executives had already decided on a title for the initiative: Strategy 2030.

Adapted from content posted on hbr.org, July 30, 2019 (product #H052ET).

I was curious to know why they chose that specific year—2030—to benchmark the work. After all, the forces affecting the company were all on different timelines: Changes in global trade were immediate concerns, while the field of robotics will have incremental advancements, disappointments, and huge breakthroughs—sometimes years apart. Had the executives chosen the year 2030 because of something unique to the company happening 10 years from today?

The reason soon became clear. They'd arbitrarily picked the year 2030, a nice round number, because it gave them a sense of control over an uncertain future. It also made for good communication. "Strategy 2030" could be easily understood by employees, customers, and competitors, and it would align with the company's messaging about its hopes for the future. Plus, when companies go through their longer-term planning processes, they often create linear timelines marked by years ending in either zeros or fives. Our brains can easily count in fives, while it takes a little extra work to count in fours or sixes.

Nice linear timelines offer a certain amount of assurance: that events can be preordained, chaos can be contained, and success can be plotted and guaranteed.[1] Of course, the real world we all inhabit is a lot messier. Regulatory actions or natural disasters are wholly outside of our control, while other factors—workforce development, operations, new product ideas—are subject to layers of decisions made throughout our organizations. As all those variables collide, they shape the horizon.

Chief strategy officers and those responsible for choosing the direction of their organizations are often asked to facilitate "visioning" meetings. This helps teams brainstorm ideas, but it isn't a substitute for critical thinking about the future. Neither are the one-, three-, or five-year strategic plans that have become a staple for most organizations, though they are useful for addressing short-term operational goals. Deep uncertainty merits deep questions, and the answers aren't necessarily tied to a fixed date in the future. Where do we want to have impact? What will it take to achieve success? How will the organization evolve to meet challenges on the horizon? These are the kinds of deep, foundational questions that are best addressed with long-term planning.

Why We Avoid Long-Term Timelines

As a quantitative futurist, my job is to investigate the future using data-driven models. My observation is that leadership teams get caught in a cycle of addressing long-term risk with rigid, short-term solutions, and in the process they invite entropy. Teams that rely on traditional linear timelines get caught in a cycle of tactical responses to what feels like constant change being foisted upon them from outside forces. Over time, those tactical responses—which take significant internal alignment and effort—drain the organization's resources and make them vulnerable to disruption.

For example, in 2001 I led a meeting with some U.S. newspaper executives to forecast the future of the news business. They, too, had already settled on a target year:

2005. This was an industry with visible disruption looming from the tech sector, where the pace of change was staggeringly fast. I already knew the cognitive bias in play (their desired year ended in a five). But I didn't anticipate the reluctance to plan beyond four years, which to the executives felt like the far future. I was concerned that any strategies we developed to confront future risk and find new opportunities would be only tactical in nature. Tactical actions without a vision of the longer-term future would result in less control over how the whole media ecosystem evolved.

To illustrate this, I pointed the executives to a new Japanese i-Mode phone I'd been using while living in Tokyo. The proto-smartphone was connected to the internet, allowed me to make purchases, and, importantly, had a camera. I asked what would happen as mobile device components dropped in price—wouldn't there be an explosion in mobile content, digital advertising, and revenue-sharing business models? Anyone would soon be able to post photos and videos to the web, and there was an entire mobile gaming ecosystem on the verge of being born.

Smartphones fell outside the scope of our 2005 timeline. While it would be a while before they posed existential risk, there was still time to build and test a long-term business model. Publishers were accustomed to executing on quarter-to-quarter strategies and didn't see the value in planning for a smartphone market that was still many years away.

Since that meeting, newspaper circulation has been on a steady decline.[2] American publishers repeatedly failed to do long-term planning, which could have included radically different revenue models for the digital age. Advertising revenue fell from $65 billion in 2000 to less than $19 billion industrywide in 2016.[3] In the United States, 1,800 newspapers closed between 2004 and 2018. Publishers made a series of short-term tactical responses (website redesigns, mobile apps) without ever developing a clear vision for the industry's evolution. Similar stories have played out across other sectors, including professional services, wired communications carriers, savings and loan banks, and manufacturing.

Use Time Cones, Not Timelines

Futurists think about time differently, and company strategists could learn from their approach. For any given uncertainty about the future—whether that's risk, opportunity, or growth—we tend to think in the short- and long-term simultaneously. To do this, I use a framework that measures certainty and charts actions, rather than simply marking the passage of time as quarters or years. That's why my timelines aren't actually lines at all—they are cones.

For every foresight project, I build a cone with four distinct categories, as depicted in figure 11-1: (1) tactics, (2) strategy, (3) vision, and (4) systems-level evolution.

I start by defining the cone's edge, using highly probable events for which there is already data or evidence. The amount of time varies for every project, organization, and industry, but typically 12 to 24 months is a good place to start. Because we can identify trends and probable events (both within a company and external to

FIGURE 11-1

A futurist's framework for strategic planning

Instead of arbitrarily assigning goals on a quarterly or yearly timeline, use a cone instead. First identify highly probable events for which there's already data or evidence, and then work outward. Each section of the cone is a strategic approach, and it encompasses the one before it until you reach major systems-level evolution at your company.

Source: Amy Webb, Future Today Institute

it), the kind of planning that can be done is *tactical* in nature, and the corresponding actions could include things like redesigning products or identifying and targeting a new customer segment.

Tactical decisions must fit into an organization's strategy. At this point in the cone, we are a little less certain of outcomes, because we're looking at the next 24 months to five years. This area is what's most familiar to strategy officers and their teams: We're describing traditional strategy and the direction the organization will take. Our actions include defining priorities, allocating resources, and making any personnel changes needed.

Lots of organizations get stuck cycling between strategy and tactics. While that process might feel like serious planning for the future, it results in a perpetual cycle of trying to catch up: to competitors, to new entrants, and to external sources of disruption.

That's why you must be willing to accept more uncertainty as you continually recalibrate your organization's vision for the future. A company's vision cannot include every detail, because there are still many unknowns. Leaders can articulate a strong vision for 10 to 15 years in the future while being open to iterating on the strategy and tactics categories as they encounter new tech trends, global events, social changes, and economic shifts. In the vision category, we formulate actions based on how the executive leadership will pursue research, where it will make investments, and how it will develop the workforce it will someday need.

But the vision for an organization must also fit into the last category: systems-level disruption that could unfold in the further future. If executive leaders do not have a strong sense of how their industry must evolve to meet the challenges of new technology, market forces, regulation, and the like, then someone else will be in a position to dictate the terms of your future. The end of the time horizons cone is very wide, since it can be impossible to calculate the probability of these kinds of events happening. So the actions taken should be describing the direction in which you hope the organization and the industry will evolve.

Unlike a traditional timeline with rigid dates and check-ins, the cone always moves forward. As you gain data and evidence and as you make progress on your actions, the beginning of the cone and your tactical category is always reset in the present day. The result, ideally, is a flexible organization that is positioned to continually iterate and respond to external developments.

Amy Webb is a quantitative futurist and professor of strategic foresight at the New York University Stern School of Business. She is the author of *The Signals Are Talking: Why Today's Fringe Is Tomorrow's Mainstream* and *The Big Nine: How the Tech Titans and Their Thinking Machines Could Warp Humanity.*

NOTES

1. Hal E. Hershfield, "Future Self-Continuity: How Conceptions of the Future Self Transform Intertemporal Choice," *Annals of the New York Academy of Sciences* 1235, no. 1 (October 2011): 30–43.

2. Michael Barthel, "Despite Subscription Surges for Largest U.S. Newspapers, Circulation and Revenue Fall for Industry Overall," Pew Research Center, June 1, 2017, https://www.pewresearch.org/fact-tank/2017/06/01/circulation-and-revenue-fall-for-newspaper-industry/.

3. Mark J. Perry, "Creative Destruction: Newspaper Ad Revenue Has Gone into a Precipitous Free Fall, and It's Probably Not Over Yet," American Enterprise Institute, August 6, 2013, https://www.aei.org/carpe-diem/creative-destruction-newspaper-ad-revenue-has-gone-into-a-precipitous-free-fall-and-its-probably-not-over-yet/.

CHAPTER 12

Ecosystem Businesses Are Changing the Rules of Strategy

by Julian Birkinshaw

Why are business ecosystems suddenly such a hot topic? It's not as though they're a new idea. The term "ecosystem" has been used in business for 20 years. Companies including Volkswagen and Toyota have been orchestrating huge networks of suppliers and distributors for more than 50 years. Lloyd's of London, the insurance

Adapted from content posted on hbr.org, August 8, 2019 (product #H053C3).

marketplace, is a classic ecosystem and was founded in the 17th century.

What's changed is that most of today's fastest-growing companies—from Amazon and Google, to Alibaba and Tencent—are *explicitly* positioning themselves as ecosystem players, as hubs within networks of customers, suppliers, and producers of complementary services. Industry observers and regulators are looking on with interest and concern. They want to understand if these companies have developed a new way of competing that might challenge the conventional view of how businesses create and capture value.

The truth is, we don't yet know if these so-called ecosystem orchestrators have an enduring advantage. For every Google or Tencent that is hugely profitable, there is a Spotify, a WeWork, or an Uber that continues to lose money. But regardless of how successful they prove to be, it's important to understand that they are playing by a different set of strategy rules than traditional firms. Rather than building moats, they are operating turnstiles.

The Old and New Rules of Competitive Advantage

Warren Buffett is famous for investing in businesses that have what strategists call "deep moats." The moat is what protects the business from competitors. Sometimes it is based on access to a scarce resource or ownership of a patent, sometimes it is based on customer loyalty and a strong brand, and sometimes it is an artifact of government regulation.

How do you build a moat? One approach is to position your business skillfully, by finding an industry with high entry barriers and then differentiating your product to keep customers hooked. The other approach is to focus on your underlying assets and capabilities and invest in those assets that are rare, valuable, and hard for competitors to imitate.

These two worldviews—market positioning and the resource-based view—have dominated how we think about competitive advantage for 40 years.

But the rapid growth of business ecosystems in recent years challenges this thinking. Most of these ecosystem orchestrators, like Google, Alibaba, and Uber, don't make the things they sell; they exist to link others together, and this makes the old positioning-based logic less relevant. And, of course, they don't have many assets, either. They create value through relationships and networks, not through physical goods or infrastructure, so arguments built around asset ownership are equally challenging. These firms are also looking to grow the market—by increasing the flow of people and goods—rather than to capture as much of the existing market as possible.

In other words, they don't care much for the moat-based logic of competitive advantage. I think a more apt metaphor for these firms may be the logic of the turnstile: They want to get as many players involved in their ecosystem as possible and to get them interacting according to rules they have shaped. Of course, there are many ways these companies make money—committees, membership fees, advertising sales, and so on—but the key point with all these business models is that they work better when the ecosystem is larger. That's why the turnstile metaphor is useful.

This shift from moats to turnstiles can be hard to grasp. For most business strategists, it is second nature to protect your existing assets and to keep competition at bay. But a pure-play orchestrator is happy to open up to competition and to share its intellectual property, as long as that keeps the ecosystem growing. Its aim is to maximize the number of people coming through the turnstile, rather than to increase the height of the fence or the width of the moat.

To help strategists understand how to put this turnstile logic into practice, here is some advice about what to focus on:

Keep customers flowing in

Most sectors have competing ecosystems—think Android versus iOS—so you need to give people a reason to participate in yours. Consider WeChat, China's dominant lifestyle and social networking app. For its first few years, WeChat was all about coming up with novel offerings, such as its Moments and Red Packets features, which drew people in. Once it was established, the app could have chosen to monetize its user base through advertising, as Facebook did. But it chose not to: Even today, users see only two ads a day, and WeChat makes its money in other ways, primarily commissions on transactions. WeChat prefers to keep the turnstiles moving by emphasizing the quality of its user experience. And it has continued to grow, with over one billion active daily users.

Give people a reason to stick around

A vibrant ecosystem is one where participants gain value in multiple ways. WeWork rents out office space to corporations, startups, and individuals in prime city locations. It could use moat-based thinking to enforce tight contracts that lock its tenants in. But it prefers to create flexible contracts that give people the option to leave, and it provides a raft of ancillary services—networking events, advice for startups, lifestyle services—that make people want to stick around. It's clear that customers like these benefits, but it's not clear yet whether WeWork will ever be able to monetize the value they are creating. Investors looking for a locked-down revenue stream will undoubtedly be steering clear of WeWork; those prepared to think big—and differently—will still see it as an opportunity.

Don't steal your partners' business

Amazon started as an online retailer, but in 2000 it opened up to selling third-party products through its marketplace. There is a delicate balance here: Amazon would like to prioritize the sales of its own products, but if it pushes those products too hard, it scares away third-party vendors and loses its attractiveness as a one-stop shop. Consider the alternative case of Alibaba, China's answer to Amazon. Unlike Amazon, Alibaba doesn't make its own products, and therefore it doesn't compete with its suppliers. As the company's website says, "We operate an ecosystem where all participants have an opportunity to prosper." Alibaba deliberately passes up some short-term money-making opportunities in pursuit of longer-term growth. As of the beginning of 2018, its third-party e-commerce businesses had grown to more than twice the size of Amazon's—and accomplished that with a staff of just 66,000 people, as compared with 550,000 at Amazon—according to the book *Ecosystem Edge* by Peter Williamson and Arnoud de Meyer.

Keep evolving

One huge benefit of being an ecosystem orchestrator is privileged access to information about the entire ecosystem. You see what's selling well, and you see how the market is evolving before others. While it might be tempting, again, to use this information to make more money in the short term, the smarter approach is to keep things moving—to open up new markets and to do this quicker than your competitors. Google illustrates this point, with its steady stream of new analytics services, as does Alibaba, with its traffic aggregation platform, Taobao Ke. WeWork isn't standing still either; in recent years it has created WeGrow, WeLive, and WeWork Labs.

The Challenges

This ecosystem-based approach to strategy isn't for everyone. As a way of working, it is inherently more stressful and chaotic than the more traditional moat-based approach. And it attracts a lot of challengers. For example, critics have suggested that WeWork's business model is a house of cards. Amazon has fallen foul of regulators for abusing its dominant position. In China, WeChat's owner, Tencent, has faced government restrictions on its growth.

To further complicate things, the split between the worlds of moats and turnstiles isn't absolute. For example, Amazon isn't just building an ecosystem—it is also operating in the brick-and-mortar world of logistics and retail. Alibaba is explicitly pushing its ecosystem strategy while also building a strong proprietary capability in artificial intelligence. Google has its own smartphone offerings alongside its search and video-sharing businesses.

The rules of competitive strategy are not getting any simpler. But a good first step to navigating them is to understand that the traditional moat-based logic of strategy doesn't work well in a world of platforms and ecosystems. By looking afresh at the way ecosystem orchestrators operate, and in particular at their fixation on increasing the flow of traffic through their turnstiles, strategists in established industries will be better positioned to compete with them.

———

Julian Birkinshaw is deputy dean and professor of strategy and entrepreneurship at the London Business School. His most recent book is *Fast/Forward: Make Your Company Fit for the Future*.

CHAPTER 13

Put Purpose at the Core of Your Strategy

by Thomas W. Malnight, Ivy Buche, and Charles Dhanaraj

Eight years ago we launched a global study of high growth in companies, investigating the importance of three strategies known to drive it: creating new markets, serving broader stakeholder needs, and changing the rules of the game. What we found surprised us. Although each of those approaches did boost growth at the organizations we studied, there was a fourth driver we hadn't considered at all: purpose.

Reprinted from *Harvard Business Review*, September–October 2019 (product #R1905D).

Companies have long been encouraged to build purpose into what they do. But usually it's talked about as an add-on—a way to create shared value, improve employee morale and commitment, give back to the community, and help the environment. But as we worked with the high-growth companies in our study and beyond, we began to recognize that many of them had moved purpose from the periphery of their strategy to its core—where, with committed leadership and financial investment, they had used it to generate sustained profitable growth, stay relevant in a rapidly changing world, and deepen ties with their stakeholders.

Two Critical Roles

In the course of our research, we talked to scores of C-level executives. They worked at 28 companies—in the United States, Europe, and India—that had had an average compound annual growth rate of 30% or more in the previous five years. What we learned from those conversations was that purpose played two important strategic roles: It helped companies *redefine the playing field*, and it allowed them to *reshape the value proposition*. And that, in turn, enabled them to overcome the challenges of slowing growth and declining profitability.

Role 1: Redefining the playing field

What's a key difference between low-growth and high-growth companies? The former spend most of their time fighting for market share on one playing field, which naturally restricts their growth potential. And because most aggressive battles take place in industries that are slowing down, gains in market share come at a high cost, often eroding profits and competitive advantage as offerings become commoditized.

High-growth companies, by contrast, don't feel limited to their current playing field. Instead, they think about whole ecosystems, where connected interests and relationships among multiple stakeholders create more opportunities. But these firms don't approach ecosystems haphazardly. They let purpose be their guide.

Consider the different strategies adopted by the two leading companies in the pet-food industry: Nestlé Purina PetCare, the largest player in North America; and Mars Petcare, the global leader. The companies have defined very similar purposes for themselves—"Better with pets" (Purina) and "A better world for pets" (Mars Petcare)—and both want to develop new products that will help customers improve their pets' health. But Purina has continued to focus on the pet-food playing field and is applying purpose in some inspiring social initiatives, whereas Mars Petcare is using purpose to propel its expansion in the broader field of pet health.

Mars Petcare, which had established a foothold in pet health with the acquisition of Banfield Pet Hospital in 2007, decided to build its presence in that arena by buying two other veterinary services: BluePearl in 2015 and VCA in 2017. Then in 2018 Mars Petcare entered the European veterinary market, buying the Swedish company AniCura, which has operations in seven European countries, and the British company Linnaeus. Those acquisitions helped Mars Petcare become Mars Inc.'s largest and fastest-growing business division.

In moving deeper into this larger ecosystem, Mars Petcare did more than just capitalize on a burgeoning industry. It also shifted its orientation beyond products to services, a radical change for an asset-heavy company that for 75 years had relied on the production and sale of goods. To succeed, the company had to build completely different core competencies and devise a new organizational structure. Many companies in this dangerously open-ended situation might have flailed, but Mars Petcare did not. It was able to pull off a transformation because it ensured that every move it made was aligned with the same core purpose. And it's not done yet: The company is now bringing that sense of purpose to efforts to expand into pet-activity monitoring with "smart" collars.

Another company that has used purpose to redefine the playing field, this time in the industrial sector, is the Finnish oil-refining firm Neste. For more than six decades Neste, founded in 1948, operated a business focused almost entirely on crude oil, but by 2009 it was struggling. The market was glutted, oil prices had dropped sharply, margins were falling, and the EU had passed new carbon-emissions legislation. During the previous two years the company's market value had shrunk by 50%.

Fighting those headwinds, the executive team, led by Neste's new CEO, Matti Lievonen, realized that the company could no longer survive on its traditional playing field. It would have to look for new opportunities in the larger ecosystem. Renewable energy could be a key driver of growth, they realized. Their purpose, they decided, should be to develop sustainable sources of energy that would help reduce emissions, and everything they did would be guided by a simple idea: "Creating responsible choices every day."

It's common for major oil companies to nod to sustainability in some way, but Lievonen quickly proved that Neste meant business, launching a bold transformation that would become a seven-year journey. Employees, customers, and investors all initially resisted the change, but Lievonen and his team were undaunted. They made major investments in infrastructure, innovated renewable technologies, focused on converting customers to green energy solutions, and, most important, engineered a fundamental change in the company's culture.

The process wasn't easy. When Lievonen was just three months into his tenure, a leading economic magazine in Finland published an article saying that he should be fired. He soldiered on, however, and by 2015 Neste had established itself as the world's largest producer of renewable fuels derived from waste and residues. A year later its comparable operating profits from renewables would surpass those of its oil-products business. In 2017 the company took yet another step by actively researching and promoting the use of waste feedstock from new sources such as algae oil, microbial oil, and tall oil pitch.

Role 2: Reshaping the value proposition

When confronted with eroding margins in a rapidly commodifying world, companies often enhance their value propositions by innovating products, services, or business models. That can bring some quick wins, but it's a transactional approach geared toward prevailing in the current arena. Because a purpose-driven approach facilitates growth in new ecosystems, it allows companies to broaden their mission, create a holistic value proposition, and deliver lifetime benefits to customers.

Companies can make this shift in three main ways: by responding to trends, building on trust, and focusing on pain points.

Responding to trends

In line with its purpose of "contributing to a safer society," Sweden's Securitas AB, a security company with 370,000 employees, has traditionally offered physical guarding services. But in the early 2010s its CEO at the time, Alf Göransson, saw that globalization, urbanization, and the increasingly networked business landscape were all changing the nature of risk—for people, operations, and business continuity. At the same time, labor was becoming more expensive, and new technologies were becoming cheaper. Given those developments, Göransson decided that Securitas could no longer "simply sell man-hours." Instead, the company had to explore new ways of using electronics to provide security. This shift, Göransson understood, was not a threat to the existing business but an opportunity to grow—as indeed it has proved to be.

In 2018 the company decided to go a step further and reshape its value proposition from reactive to predictive security, a plan that once again built on the company's core purpose. Under the leadership of Göransson's successor, Magnus Ahlqvist, the firm strengthened its electronic security business by acquiring a number of companies, investing heavily in modernizing and integrating back-office systems, and training its guards in remote surveillance, digital reporting, and efficient response. That allowed Securitas to offer bundled, customized security solutions—encompassing physical guarding, electronic security, and risk management—that provided a much-enhanced level of protection at an optimized cost. By expanding its value proposition in this way, Securitas has been able to strengthen client relationships and significantly increase its margins for the solutions business. From 2012 to 2018 the company's sales of security solutions and electronic security also increased, from 6% of total revenue to 20%.

Building on trust

When Mahindra Finance, the financial services arm of the Mahindra Group, a $20 billion Indian conglomerate, wanted to define its value proposition, it looked to its parent company's longtime purpose-driven strategy of improving customers' lives—encapsulated in 2010 by the simple motto "Rise." It's a word that the company's third-generation leader, Anand Mahindra, expects will inspire employees to accept no limits, think alternatively, and drive positive change.

In keeping with that strategy, Mahindra Finance decided to target its core offering, vehicle financing, to rural areas, where it could—as Rajeev Dubey, the group head of HR, put it to us—"address the unmet needs of underserved customers in an underpenetrated market."

That meant that the company had to figure out how to determine the creditworthiness of customers who were mostly poor, illiterate, and unbanked, with no identity documents, no collateral, and cash flows that were often impacted by monsoons. To do that, the company had to develop completely new ways to handle loan design, repayment terms, customer approval, branch locations, and disbursement and collection in cash. Not only that, but it had to figure out how to recruit workers who could speak local dialects, assess local situations, and operate under a decentralized model of decision making.

Remarkably, the company managed to do all those things and established a preliminary level of trust with its customers. It then stretched its value proposition to help farmers and other customers obtain insurance for their tractors, lives, and health. In a country where insurance penetration is abysmally low (about 3.5%), this was no small feat, especially since rural residents didn't easily part with any minuscule monthly surplus they had, even if it was to secure their livelihood.

Then Mahindra Finance extended its purpose-driven efforts to housing finance, another arena in which it recognized that it could help its rural customers rise above their circumstances. For most of those people, securing loans for housing was difficult in the extreme. Banks offered loans at an interest rate of about 10% but demanded documentation most rural residents couldn't provide. Moneylenders offered instant financing but charged interest rates of about 40%. Recognizing an opportunity, Mahindra Finance decided to play at the intermediate level, offering customized home loans at rates of about 14%, an option that appealed to its growing base of customers. And when some of those customers developed successful small agribusinesses, they began looking for working-capital loans, equipment loans, project finance, and so on—more unmet needs that Mahindra Finance could address. So it extended its value proposition again, into the small-to-medium-enterprise arena, offering finance and asset-management services.

Throughout its expansion, Mahindra Finance was guided by its goal of helping rural citizens improve their lives. The company identified and committed itself to value propositions that allowed it to deepen its relationship with its customers, which in turn created additional streams of revenue and profits. Today Mahindra Finance is India's largest rural nonbanking financial company, serving 50% of villages and 6 million customers.

Focusing on pain points

We've already seen how Mars Petcare's health care value proposition led to direct connections with pet owners at multiple touchpoints. Having established them, the company looked for other ways to create "a better world for pets." How could it come up with a value proposition that would make pet ownership a seamless, convenient, and attractive experience?

The answer was by investing in technology to help address one of the biggest concerns of pet owners: *preventing* health problems. In 2016 the company acquired

Whistle, the San Francisco–based maker of a connected collar for activity monitoring and location tracking—a kind of Fitbit for dogs. Teaming the device up with its Banfield Pet Hospital unit, the company launched the Pet Insight Project, a three-year longitudinal study that aims to enroll 200,000 dogs in the United States. By combining machine learning, data science, and deep veterinary expertise, the project seeks to understand when behavior may signal a change in a pet's health and how owners can partner with their veterinarians on individualized diagnostics and treatments for their pets.

Developing a Purpose

Leaders and companies that have effectively defined corporate purpose typically have done so with one of two approaches: *retrospective* or *prospective.*

The retrospective approach builds on a firm's existing reason for being. It requires that you look back, codify organizational and cultural DNA, and make sense of the firm's past. The focus of the discovery process is internal. Where have we come from? How did we get here? What makes us unique to all stakeholders? Where does our DNA open up future opportunities we believe in? These are the kinds of questions leaders have to ask.

Anand Mahindra very successfully employed this tactic at the Mahindra Group. First he looked back at his 30 years at the company and at the values that had guided him as its leader. Then he delved into the psyche of the organization by conducting internal surveys of managers at all levels. He also did ethnographic research in seven countries to identify themes that resonated with his company's multinational, cross-cultural employee base. The

IS PURPOSE AT THE CORE OF YOUR STRATEGY?

Not unless you answer yes to all five questions below.

1. Does purpose contribute to increasing your company's growth and profitability today?

2. Does purpose significantly influence your strategic decisions and investment choices?

3. Does purpose shape your core value proposition?

4. Does purpose affect how you build and manage your organizational capabilities?

5. Is purpose on the agenda of your leadership team every time you meet?

process took three years, but ultimately Mahindra arrived at "Rise," which, he realized, had been fundamental to the company from its inception. "'Rise' is not a clever tagline," he has said. "We were already living and operating this way."

The prospective approach, on the other hand, reshapes your reason for being. It requires you to look forward, take stock of the broader ecosystem in which you want to work, and assess your potential for impact in it. The idea is to make sense of the future and then start gearing your organization for it. The focus is external, and leaders have to ask a different set of questions: Where can we go? Which trends affect our business? What new needs, opportunities, and challenges lie ahead? What role can we play that will open up future opportunities for ourselves that we believe in?

The prospective approach can be particularly useful for new CEOs. In 2018, when Magnus Ahlqvist took charge at Securitas, he spearheaded a "purpose workstream" to capture aspirations for the company from the ground up. He asked all his business-unit leaders to run "listening workshops" (with groups of employees from diverse functions, levels, age groups, genders, and backgrounds), which were held over six months. At the end of that period, the findings were collated and analyzed. Among the discoveries: Employees had a vision of transforming the company from a *service provider* to a *trusted adviser*. That shift would require anticipating and responding to security issues instead of relying on the legacy methods of observing and reporting. So employee input helped executives refine the firm's predictive-security strategy.

Implementing a Purpose-Driven Strategy

Our research shows that a compelling purpose clarifies what a company stands for, provides an impetus for action, and is aspirational. But some purpose statements are so generic that they could apply to any company (like Nissan's, "Enriching people's lives"), while others provide only a narrow description of the company's existing businesses (like Wells Fargo's, "We want to satisfy our customers' financial needs and help them succeed financially"). Even if organizations do manage to define their purpose well, they often don't properly translate it into action—or do anything at all to fulfill it. In those cases the purpose becomes nothing more than nice-sounding words on a wall.

Leaders need to think hard about how to make purpose central to their strategy. The two best tactics for doing that are to *transform the leadership agenda* and to *disseminate purpose throughout the organization.*

Consider Mars Petcare again. In 2015 its president, Poul Weihrauch, significantly altered the composition and focus of the leadership team. Its new collective agenda, he declared, would go beyond the performance of individual businesses; it would include generating "multiplier effects" among the businesses (such as between pet food and pet health) and increasing their contributions to creating a better world for pets.

In keeping with that principle, Weihrauch had the company adopt an "outside-in" approach to meeting stakeholder needs. As part of this effort, in 2018 Mars Petcare launched two new programs to support startups innovating in pet care: Leap Venture Studio, a business accelerator formed in partnership with Michelson Found Animals and R/GA; and Companion Fund, a $100 million venture-capital fund in partnership with Digitalis Ventures. In announcing these initiatives the company declared that its ambition was "to become a partner of choice for everyone willing to change the rules of the game in pet care."

Revising a leadership agenda and restructuring an organization are arguably easier at a privately held company like Mars Petcare than at a publicly held one. But Finland's Neste is public, with a major stake held by the government, and it has managed to do both things very effectively.

Neste faced an uphill battle when it decided to move into renewables. The company had to build new capabilities while confronting strong opposition from many employees who didn't buy into the change in direction. About 10% of them left during the first year of the strategy's implementation. Painful as it was, it proved to be a positive development, since the company could not have forged ahead with people who didn't believe in its new purpose.

And forge ahead it did. Neste put in place a new top management team, mobilized its 1,500 R&D engineers, innovated patented renewable technology, and invested €2 billion in building new refineries.

The shift also raised a big question for Neste. How could it change its organizational mindset from *volume* to *value* selling—which entailed convincing customers that its clean fuels would be better for them in the long run? That shift meant going beyond wholesalers to work directly with the distributors and even the distributors' customers. The new leadership team realized that a much higher level of collaboration among business segments and functions was imperative. Winning deals was no longer the sole responsibility of the sales department. The expertise of the whole organization—product knowledge, marketing, finance, taxation—would be required to understand the specific needs of customers like airlines and bus fleets. So Neste engineered a major reorganization and created a matrix structure, in the process rotating about 25% of senior managers and about 50% of upper professionals into new positions. Targets and incentive plans became cross-functional, designed to build capabilities both within and across businesses. And at every step, purpose helped everybody in the company understand the "why" (the business environment's increasing emphasis on sustainability), the "what" (value-creation programs offering renewable solutions to customers, which in turn generated higher margins for Neste), and the "how" (changing from a sales organization to a key-account management model with dedicated people responsible for strategic customers).

The process worked. Neste is now a leader in the renewables industry, and the world is starting to pay attention. In 2015, for example, Google and UPS began partnering with the company to reduce their carbon emissions, as did several cities in California, among them San Francisco and Oakland. In 2018, Forbes ranked Neste second on its Global 100 list of the world's most-sustainable companies.

Benefits on the Soft Side

Purpose can also help with the soft side of management—the people-related aspects of running a business, which so often prove to be the undoing of leaders. By putting purpose at the core of strategy, firms can realize three specific benefits: more-unified organizations, more-motivated stakeholders, and a broader positive impact on society.

Unifying the organization

When companies pursue dramatic change and move into larger ecosystems, as both Mars Petcare and Securitas have done, it's unsettling for employees. Why does a pet-food company need to develop a platform to support technology startups? Why does an on-site guarding company want to provide electronic security services that could, over time, make the physical presence of guards redundant? Purpose helps employees understand the whys and get on board with the new direction.

Motivating stakeholders

According to the Edelman trust barometer, distrust of government, businesses, the media, and NGOs is now pervasive. At the same time, more than ever, employees, especially Millennials, want to work for organizations that can be trusted to contribute to a higher cause. And when customers, suppliers, and other stakeholders see that a company has a strong higher purpose, they are more likely to trust it and more motivated to interact with it.

Broadening impact

Strategy involves exploring some fundamental questions. Why are we in this business? What value can we bring? What role does my unit play within the bigger portfolio? Purpose creates a basis for answering those questions and defining how each unit will contribute to the organization and to society as a whole. This focus on collective objectives, in turn, opens up many more opportunities to improve growth and profitability today and in the future.

Conclusion

The approach to purpose that we're recommending cannot be a one-off effort. Leaders need to constantly assess how purpose can guide strategy, and they need to be willing to adjust or redefine this relationship as conditions change. That demands a new kind of sustained focus, but the advantages it can confer are legion.

Thomas W. Malnight is a professor of strategy and faculty director of the Business Transformation Initiative at IMD in Lausanne, Switzerland. He is a coauthor of *Ready? The 3Rs of Preparing Your Organization for the Future.* **Ivy Buche** is an associate director of the Business Transformation Initiative at IMD. **Charles Dhanaraj** is the H. F. "Gerry" Lenfest Professor of Strategy at Temple University's Fox School of Business, where he is also the founding executive director of the Translational Research Center.

Test Your Strategic Choices

CHAPTER 14

Four Ways to Pressure-Test Your Strategy

by Rick Lynch and Jay Galeota

Every leader wants to avoid major strategic mistakes, but, in a complex world, it's hard to anticipate all the forces that might impact your goal. It's vital to find weaknesses in your strategies *before* you implement them—and to develop a rigorous process to do so.

The ability to poke holes in one's own strategies is something the U.S. military has practiced and refined over centuries. Rick served in the U.S. Army for 35 years,

---

Adapted from "4 Ways to Pressure-Test Strategic Decisions, Inspired by the U.S. Military" on hbr.org, October 30, 2018 (product #H04ML7).

retiring as a lieutenant general, and has seen this first-hand. In the heat of battle, strategic planning that's incomplete or simply wrong causes leaders to revert to on-the-spot decision making. While sometimes necessary, making it up as you go is more often associated with failure—and loss of life—and is often a symptom of ineffective or inaccurate anticipation of competitive moves or environmental shifts.

The same is true in business, and the techniques the military has honed can help executives anticipate problems and change course when necessary.

Build Situational Awareness

Simply put, situational awareness is achieved after a soldier has deliberately assessed an environment from various vantage points and has ensured that all potential perspectives have been captured.

In the business world, things are fuzzier—there are no landscapes, buildings, or troop movements to scan. But it's still crucial to make sense of the environments in which we operate and foresee how different factors will affect our decisions.

One way to build one's situational awareness is to talk through alternate realities. Although this sounds like science fiction, alternate realities are basically hypotheticals. We think X will happen, but what if Y or Z does instead?

At Merck, where Jay served as chief strategy and business development officer and president of emerging businesses, "alternate realities" were used to prevent "team think," which frequently occurs when organizations believe the conventional view of a situation is the correct one.

To develop better situational awareness, start by forming teams and tasking them to develop alternatives based on different views of the same situation. For example, what if new competitors enter the market earlier than expected? What could they do that would surprise or outmaneuver us? What if they are delayed; what types of things might they do to try to recover and penetrate the market more quickly? Could any of their actions be extreme or desperate? What actions could and should our team consider to mitigate or blunt the risk in these alternate scenarios?

The next step is to compare these hypotheticals collectively and then determine what countermeasures will have the most impact.

Most importantly, make sure to consider specific "triggers" that would indicate one or more of the alternative scenarios is unfolding. Agreeing on these triggers up front is useful because they prospectively define specific thresholds for change in action or direction. Once identified, you should track these triggers regularly on a dashboard that all senior team members see. This eliminates or greatly reduces debate when course changes become necessary and urgent. Then, make sure that group leaders complete a situational awareness assessment regularly and discuss the alternative scenarios and triggers during each business review.

Small investments of time can result in new insights about your organization's readiness, and your leaders' acumen, that would have gone unnoticed until a crisis.

Develop an Outside-In Perspective

This is another technique that's routine in the military and can highlight unique but under-leveraged capabilities or untapped sources of competitive advantage. Think of aviation. For a long time, the military used aircrafts primarily to increase visibility of topography and troop movements, but starting in the early 1900s, the military began using planes to deliver ordnance and conduct warfare. What are your organization's aircraft?

Frequently, these are ancillary assets or capabilities that are often considered to be a "cost of doing business." These could include a controlled global supply chain, distinct abilities to test compounds, proprietary communication channels with key constituents, unique manufacturing machinery, and so on. Think to yourself: In future scenarios, could any of these become new lines of business? If your environment changes unexpectedly could any of them help you to adapt?

In companies, an outside-in perspective can help shape an honest view of your organization's strengths (and weaknesses). Customers can be a great source for this. Forming a strategic advisory council is another option.

Game It Out

Another practice is war-gaming, and there is often no substitute for putting real people into the mix to see how they react. Even complex AI simulation, while helpful, can lack the variability and ingenuity of human creativity. The U.S. military has become an expert in preparing for combat operations using war games. Most notable is the establishment of the National Training Center in the Mohave Desert in California where the U.S. Army conducts live, force-on-force battles to refine its capabilities.

At Merck, war-gaming exercises around critical decisions were used frequently. The process was as follows: Assign high-performing managers to lead "opposing" teams made up of individuals with expertise across relevant functional areas. Before the exercise, prepare a background that outlines the general challenge and provides specific information and data. Task the line area most responsible for the situation with organizing and leading the overall exercise—and make sure that each group presents its findings at the end. Incentivizing "opposing" teams for success will help ensure a robust simulation. For example, consider inviting a senior leader to judge the readout and offer a cash bonus, recognition, or both for the winning team.

Form Diverse, Strategic Groups

Finally, form strategic initiatives groups, and populate them with people who can analyze problems from various perspectives.

At Merck, the strategic initiative group often came up with alternate decisions and actions on key business issues. In one case, the choice to position a new product as second-line treatment versus trying to displace a well-accepted initial therapy turned out to be uniquely advantageous, helping achieve a launch that far exceeded expectations.

Looking at your strategy in a variety of ways can help you see where there might be issues before it's too late to make changes. Learning from the experience of the military and applying these approaches to your own business can help you assess your weaknesses and adjust before implementation.

Rick Lynch served in the U.S. Army for 35 years, retiring as a lieutenant general. His last job in the Army was commanding all of the U.S. Army installations (163 worldwide) with a workforce of 120,000 and an annual budget of $15 billion. He is the author of *Adapt or Die: Battle-tested Principles for Leaders* and *Work Hard, Pray Hard: The Power of Faith in Action.* **Jay Galeota** is the president and CEO of Inheris Biopharma, Inc. He was the chief strategy and business development officer and president of emerging businesses at Merck and president of G&W Laboratories, Inc., prior to his current role.

CHAPTER 15

Which Strategy "Comfort Traps" Are You Falling Into?

by Roger L. Martin

Faced with an unpredictable future, strategy makers often fall into three traps:

1. **Strategic planning:** They create a long list of to-dos without having a strategy to carry out.

2. **Cost-based thinking:** They try to model revenue (which is hard to nail down) the same

Adapted from content (assessment) posted on hbr.org, May 2014, https://hbr.org/web/assessment/2014/05/which-strategy-comfort -traps-are-you-falling-into.

way they model costs (which are much easier to predict).

3. **Self-referential frameworks:** They focus on the company's existing strengths and its ability to quickly copy rivals' moves instead of finding a new source of competitive advantage.

Though understandable, these avoidance behaviors are dangerous. If creating strategy feels comfortable, chances are you're not really doing it.

Answer the following questions to find out which traps (if any) you've fallen into and how to get out of them. "No" responses show that you're on the right track. But if you find yourself answering "yes" to any of these questions, you may have a problem. Use the tips below to remedy the situation.

Comfort Trap 1: Strategic Planning

1. Is your strategic plan a long document (50-plus pages) that lists many functional, product, and geographic initiatives?

Problem: A long planning document may feel rigorous, but the longer it is, the more it will distract you from the harder strategic work of finding ways to acquire and retain customers. Listing a bunch of things that the company plans to do is not the same as creating a strategy.

Remedy: Set the plan aside and ask yourself, "Of all the places we could 'play' in the marketplace, where will we play? And how will we beat competitors there?" One page should be sufficient, and five pages the absolute maximum. Initiatives are an important component of a good strategy, but they must be clearly linked to "where to play" and "how to win" choices. Make those choices first and then work out a plan that supports them. (To read more about where to play and how to win, flip back to chapter 9.)

2. Is it difficult to identify any explicit choices that show what the company will not do?

Problem: If you haven't specified what the company will not do, you haven't effectively specified what it will, which means you don't have a strategy.

Remedy: Identify a number of places you won't play. Once you've defined enough of that territory, you'll be able to describe where you will play with greater precision.

3. Does the plan spend more time describing what will happen in the first one to two years than it spends on years five to 10?

Problem: What you have is really just a budget expressed in prose, not a strategy.

Remedy: Pick five years as the focus of your strategy. Where does the company want to play—and how does it want to win—five years from now? After you've determined that, make the next four years the steps you need to take to achieve your five-year target.

Comfort Trap 2: Cost-Based Thinking

**4. Does your strategic plan review costs in more
detail than revenue?**

Problem: You are spending more time on the easier
thing to do.

Remedy: Spend two to three times as many person-
hours modeling revenue as modeling costs. Anybody
can model costs. It takes real effort and skill to model
revenue, because it's controlled by customers, not the
company. Revenue modeling necessitates a deep understanding of customer needs.

**5. Is it difficult to see any link between revenue
predictions and the value proposition?**

Problem: If the link isn't obvious, then the revenue
predictions aren't worth the paper they're printed on.
Most revenue projections are just extrapolations from
past revenue, even though competition is notoriously
unstable.

Remedy: Look to the future, not the past. Base your projections on how well the value proposition suits customers where the company has chosen to play.

**6. Do you treat the predictability of revenue as
equivalent to the predictability of costs and model
them in a similar fashion?**

Problem: Because revenue is determined by customer behavior, it's much harder and messier to predict than costs, which are largely under the company's control. If you model them the same way, you'll end up with grossly inaccurate revenue projections.

Remedy: To model revenue, start by predicting customers' choices rather than deciding what the company wants to do. When creating strategies and budgets, assume a greater range of error for revenue than for costs. Whereas costs might have an error range of plus or minus 5%, for example, a realistic error range for revenue might be plus or minus 20%.

Comfort Trap 3: Self-Referential Frameworks

7. Does the strategic plan avoid making concrete predictions about the future of competition in your industry?

Problem: You may think you're applying the concept of "emergent strategy" by avoiding commitment to a predicted future. But to have a strategy of any kind, a company must develop a model of how it thinks competition will look five to 10 years down the road. Without that model, the company can't make strategic "where to play" and "how to win" choices.

Remedy: Make a prediction about the future even if it's likely to be only partially accurate. Your vision of the future should inform the strategic bets you're placing now.

8. Does the strategic plan recommend "fast following" market innovators?

Problem: Fast following is not strategy but the abdication of strategy. The companies least likely to be successful at it are those that make it their goal. They don't know what to follow fast and when to start following.

Remedy: Don't fast follow. Choose where to play and how to win; then watch what happens, learn, and adjust your choices accordingly.

9. Does the strategic plan proudly affirm existing capabilities that are difficult to link to particular customer needs?

Problem: If a company luxuriates in its existing capabilities, it will reinforce an internal, producer-focused mentality. It will be hard-pressed to become or stay customer-focused.

Remedy: Specify which capabilities must be built or maintained to produce the winning value proposition for the targeted set of customers. Capabilities matter only to the extent that they help your company meet customers' needs better than rivals do where you've decided to play.

As you pursue and refine your strategy, continue to ask hard questions. Also, ask someone else who knows your organization well to take the assessment. You don't want to fool yourself into thinking that your strategy is flawless when it might not be. "No" responses show that you're on the right track.

Roger L. Martin is professor emeritus and former dean of the Rotman School of Management at the University of Toronto. He is a coauthor of *Creating Great Choices: A Leader's Guide to Integrative Thinking* (Harvard Business Review Press, 2017).

CHAPTER 16

Identify the New Capabilities You Need

by Ron Ashkenas and Logan Chandler

While strategic plans identify what your organization should do differently, very few provide a road map for how to build the skills, knowledge, and processes needed to carry out and sustain the critical changes. But without building these capabilities, it's very difficult to achieve the results you want.

For example, a multiproduct technology firm we advised laid out a strategy to significantly increase business

---

Adapted from "Your Strategy Won't Work If You Don't Identify the New Capabilities You Need" on hbr.org, November 1, 2017 (product #H03ZPZ).

with its large enterprise customers by creating single points of contact and focusing on providing solutions as opposed to delivering products. The strategy was sound, but making it happen required many new capabilities: Dozens of sales people had to learn new approaches to selling and relationship building, different sales divisions needed to share information and collaborate, new roles for coordinating enterprise accounts had to be created, financial information had to be presented and analyzed differently, and so on. These changes meant that hundreds of people in the company had to work differently in some way—but the plan said nothing about developing capabilities. So despite general agreement that the strategy made sense, the missing capabilities made it impossible to carry out.

Capabilities lie at the heart an organization's ability to achieve results, so it's hardly a surprise that different results require different capabilities. But strategic plans often get this simple equation wrong, for one of two reasons.

First, many strategic planners and senior executives assume that if the strategy is logical then people will figure out what to do and don't build capabilities development into their plans at all. And yes, every organization has people who are highly adaptable, learn quickly, and can operate in this mode. Unfortunately, they often comprise a small group, and leaders end up over-relying on these individuals to tackle challenging execution assignments. And since these few people can't do it all, the efforts founder.

At the other extreme, some planners like to be prescriptive and can spend significant resources mapping out in great detail what everyone should do differently. But a paint-by-numbers approach to strengthening organizational capabilities rarely works. Developing capabilities requires experimentation, trial and error, and iterative learning to figure out what will work in each organization's unique culture, functional structure, and environment. Faced with lengthy lists of best practices and new processes that don't match reality, teams simply give up and revert to old patterns of behavior.

Overcoming these pitfalls requires thinking of capability development in a different way: as an integral part of strategic execution. The key is to link each strategic priority to the capabilities needed to drive that opportunity and to frame accountability for each strategic priority around both results and capability development. Let's look at one company that we helped take this approach.

When leaders of Rich Products, a global food manufacturer, launched a strategic initiative focused on accelerating innovation, they recognized that helping the organization simultaneously strengthen its innovation "muscles" was critical to addressing the challenge. So, while some work focused on innovation strategy—the customary task of identifying where the company should place innovation bets—equal attention was paid to understanding the capabilities needed to execute the strategy. Formal diagnostics and substantive discussions across the organization generated a clear picture of the specific capabilities that would need to be strengthened if the organization was to achieve its innovation targets in the necessary time frame.

As teams were chartered to pursue promising opportunities, they were also tasked with developing specific capabilities that were critical to the innovation strategy. For instance, a team trying to introduce a promising cooking technology was also tasked with learning how to do effective customer immersions, a key capability gap for the organization. Another team trying to launch a new platform of food products was also made responsible for finding ways to strengthen new product introductions. In each case, leadership regularly reviewed progress with teams, not just on the business outcomes but also on what each team was learning about its assigned skill. As successive phases of this work took place, teams brought what they learned to new iterations and new teams, helping to scale and sustain the development of these capabilities. Now Rich Products is embedding this approach in its ongoing multiyear innovation efforts.

The technology company mentioned in the beginning also eventually used this approach but in a slightly different way. They created three small teams of sales, HR, and finance people and challenged them to increase revenues from three enterprise accounts while also figuring out what capabilities they needed to be successful. The three teams then began to test new ways of working with their actual clients, configured different financial reports, carved out new roles for team members, and more. As they proceeded, they met together regularly to share what they were learning. Eventually, the three teams developed a successful model for how to work with their accounts and increase sales results. Each team then mentored two other new groups and helped them learn what worked for their clients—while all the teams continued to share best practices and refine the model. Over the next two years this iterative cascade approach continued until 150 of the largest accounts were being handled in this new way.

As these examples illustrate, combining capability development with strategy execution does not need to be a complex undertaking. The key is to make capability learning as overt and intentional as possible. This will allow you to build organization muscle while getting business results.

Ron Ashkenas is a coauthor of the *Harvard Business Review Leader's Handbook* and a partner emeritus at Schaffer Consulting. His previous books include *The Boundaryless Organization, The GE Work-Out,* and *Simply Effective*. **Logan Chandler** is a senior partner with Schaffer Consulting and the coauthor of the *Harvard Business Review* article "Off-Sites That Work."

CHAPTER 17

A Simple Way to Test Your Company's Strategic Alignment

by Jonathan Trevor and Barry Varcoe

There is no universal or one-size-fits-all prescription for a winning business. But corporate leaders today seem to agree that strategic alignment is high on the list.

Strategic alignment, for us, means that all elements of a business—including the market strategy and the

---

Adapted from content posted on hbr.org, May 16, 2016 (product #H02VVA).

way the company itself is organized—are arranged in such a way as to best support the fulfillment of its long-term purpose. While a company's purpose generally doesn't change, strategies and organizational structures do, which can make chasing "alignment" between strategy and the organization feel like chasing an elusive will-o'-the-wisp.

As if that weren't tough enough, another challenge for corporate leaders is how to make sense of strategic alignment at *both* the team/business-unit level (or division or department, however it is classified) *and* at the enterprise level. (See the sidebar "Is Anyone in Your Company Paying Attention to Strategic Alignment?")

Yet it is possible. For example, as it grew, Facebook found that its early "move fast and break things" culture had to be funneled into focused technical teams and product groups to make its product development process faster and less erratic and for it to have a chance of meeting the demands of its new public shareholders following its IPO. The current mantra is "move fast with stable infrastructure," which speaks to the organizational design challenge of operating at scale in a fickle and volatile world.

There is a simple test you can perform to start an honest conversation about strategy and organizational effectiveness where you work. Think of your company in its entirety or perhaps select a strategically important element of it, such as a growth area upon which future success depends or its primary source of income, and consider the following two questions:

1. **How well does your business strategy support the fulfillment of your company's purpose?** Purpose

is *what* the business is trying to achieve. Strategy is *how* the business will achieve it. Purpose is enduring—it is the north star toward which the company should point. Strategy involves choices about what products and services to offer, which markets to serve, and how the company should best set itself apart from rivals for competitive advantage. Think of your own business and ask yourself, using a scale of 1–100, *How well does our strategy support the fulfillment of our purpose?* (If you are unclear on your company's strategic priorities, or its purpose, then the likelihood is that it does not.)

2. **How well does your organization support the achievement of your business strategy?** "Organization," as we're using it here, includes all of the required capabilities, resources (including human), and management systems necessary to implement your strategy. For instance, if your company seeks to beat competitors through superior customer service, is this reflected in the day-to-day behavior of staff and their interactions with customers? If innovation is a key strategic priority, does your organizational structure enable creative collaboration, risk-taking, and knowledge sharing? To maintain strategic alignment, a company's people, culture, structure, and processes have to flex and change as the strategy itself shifts. The symptoms of poor alignment are often obvious, especially to those who work in the company,

IS ANYONE IN YOUR COMPANY PAYING ATTENTION TO STRATEGIC ALIGNMENT?

by Jonathan Trevor

In my research and consultancy with companies, I observe that, oftentimes, no individual or group is functionally responsible for overseeing the arrangement of their company from end to end. Multiple different individuals and groups are responsible for different components of the value chain that makes up their company's design, and they are often not as joined up as they should be. All too often, individual leaders seek— indeed are incentivized—to protect and optimize their own domains and find themselves locked in energy-sapping internal turf wars, rather than working with peers to align and improve across the entire enterprise.

So, who should be responsible for ensuring your company is as *strategically aligned* as it can be? Consider these questions for your own company:

- *Who* at the enterprise level in your company is responsible for ensuring it's as strategically aligned as possible? Is their focus and behavior consistent with this responsibility, or is it merely an addition to their overriding day job? Is it the responsibility of your company's most senior managers, or should it be a more distributed responsibility? How much and how often is time devoted in your company to revisiting its core organizing principles and discussing how to build capability for tomorrow's customer, versus focusing on today's business?

- *How* is your company's leadership making informed decisions about the arrangement of your company as a complex system of many moving and interconnected parts—including organizational capabilities, resources, and management systems—all aimed at fulfilling one overarching purpose? What frameworks and information do your leaders require to ask good questions, have better conversations, and make robust strategic and organizational choices?

- *What* capabilities do your enterprise-level leaders require to be effective at aligning your company to ensure it is fit for its purpose? Leaders I've worked with who take on the challenge of strategic alignment describe themselves as needing to be "multi-everything" in outlook and ability. This means being *multilevel*, or being capable of enterprise-level thinking; *multidisciplinary*, being "T-shaped," or possessing generalist and specialist knowledge ranging across the business; *multinational*, having no geographical or cultural bias in scope or decision making; *multistakeholder*, understanding the company from multiple perspectives and interests; and *multiphased*, choosing to think in the near-, medium-, and long-term despite pressure for immediate results.

If there are no obvious answers to these questions, then there is a good chance that nobody is paying enough attention to strategic alignment in your company. If that's the case, you urgently need to address this gap in leadership focus and capability.

Adapted from content posted on hbr.org, January 12, 2018 (product #H043U2).

but also to customers who do not experience the service they expect from a company's branding and advertising. Using the same 1–100 scale, ask yourself: *How well does our organization support the achievement of our strategy?* If your organization is incapable of delivering its strategy, the strategy is effectively worthless and your company's purpose will go more or less unfulfilled.

Your answers to both questions can be plotted on the matrix in figure 17-1. Each state poses a different leadership challenge. (Across all four, however, we're assuming that the purpose itself is viable and has the potential to be successful.)

FIGURE 17-1

The best companies are the best aligned

Strategy, purpose, and organizational capabilities must be in sync.

How aligned is your strategy with your organizational capabilities?

Very best chance of winning: Companies that score highly on both scales stand the very best chance of winning in their competitive field. But alignment manifests itself in more than just superior financial performance. It also leads to a more positive work climate, above-average staff engagement, a strong commitment to values, and few(er) energy-sapping turf wars and in-fighting. There is a buzz, no matter what the type of business, because people value being part of a company that is winning.

ARM is possibly one of the best-performing companies you've never heard of. Its microprocessors are used in over 95% of the world's smart devices, including iOS and Android smartphones and tablets. Superior technical innovation is at the heart of its strategy and its organizational design. ARM organizes purposefully for innovation by maximizing opportunities for knowledge sharing and collaboration throughout its entire ecosystem comprising thousands of external partners. Its core staff of only 3,500 based mostly in Cambridge (UK) shares a singular purpose and set of values that supersede functions, occupations, and roles. There are few barriers to spontaneous collaboration among technical teams.

Best of intentions, but incapable: Companies that score highly on the purpose and strategy alignment scale, but low on the strategy and organization scale, are more or less incapable of implementing their strategy as intended. The performance penalty may be manifest in poor customer attraction and retention, higher-than-expected costs, organizational dysfunctions, or simple financial underperformance.

Like many leading international banks in recent years, Barclays has been subjected to strong criticism of its culture, governance, and risky behavior that contributed to the 2008 financial crisis. A series of scandals, such as foreign exchange fixing, has resulted in it receiving record fines, regulatory scrutiny, and highly negative publicity. A report commissioned by Barclays in 2013 revealed a corporate culture that wasn't fit for purpose, tending to "favor transactions over relationships, the short term over sustainability, and financial over other business purposes."[1] It further revealed a complex and siloed organization, with competing operating assumptions, values, and practices across the group. The result was a fertile environment for reckless and risky employee behavior running contrary to the overarching vision and values of the enterprise.

Boldly going nowhere: Businesses that have strong alignment between their strategy and organization but weak alignment between strategy and purpose are classed as "boldly going nowhere." In our experience, there are many capable businesses with great people that lack a coherent, overarching purpose that helps guide shifts in strategy. The result is a company that becomes less and less capable over time as customers move on and talented employees depart for new pastures. Kodak is a famous example of a terrifically capable blue-chip business brought low by confusion about how best to fulfil its purpose in the digital world. Although it developed digital photographic technology, too many people in the company focused on the core organizational competence of film. Instead of seeing digital cameras as a new way to execute on the organizational purpose of capturing "Kodak moments," they hewed to their existing, film-centric strategy. That left them out of sync with the changing preferences of consumers for digital media and instant sharing.

Not long for this world: Companies that score low on both scales are in crisis, even if it isn't immediately obvious. Their strategies do not—cannot—fulfill their larger purpose, because they fail to effectively address customer preference, market conditions, and competitor capability. Equally significant, their organization is incapable of delivering against strategic priorities.

The fall can come quickly. Royal Bank of Scotland (RBS) was a flagship bank, feted for its stellar financial performance. It grew rapidly in the late '90s and early 2000s, transforming itself from a regional Scottish bank into a national British bank with the acquisition of National Westminster Bank in 2000, finally and fleetingly becoming a global universal bank with the acquisition of ABN Amro in 2007. At its peak, RBS employed 170,000 people and operated in more than 50 countries with annual profits of £10.3 billion. In 2008, however, RBS failed spectacularly and was nationalized by the UK government to prevent its collapse.

Many have speculated since about failures of its leadership under its bullish former CEO, Fred Goodwin. Goodwin was notoriously combative, with a "Fred says" autocratic management style. RBS was also famous for its "strategy of not having a strategy," being largely opportunistic and relying upon aggressive plays, agility, and audacity to outpace peers. Supercharged inorganic growth—especially the acquisition of ABN Amro—meant that RBS grew very large, very quickly, with multiple different operating structures and subcultures. RBS outgrew the ability of its command-and-control leadership structure to effectively govern complex and diversified activities across international operations. Many poor business decisions resulted in an accumulation of unsustainable toxic debt. Almost a decade on from its nationalization, RBS still remains on life support provided by UK taxpayers and has yet to return to sustainable profit, posting yet another loss in 2015 that has more or less wiped out the equivalent of all the public money invested since its downfall.

How does your company score? What does it tell you about how you perceive the effectiveness of your strategy, or your organization? Consider further: *Why* have you rated your business the way you have, and, if accurate, *what* are the consequences for performance in future?

Jonathan Trevor is an associate professor of management practice at Oxford University's Saïd Business School. **Barry Varcoe** is global director of real estate and facilities at the Open Society Foundations.

NOTE

1. Anthony Salz, "Salz Review: An Independent Review of Barclays' Business Practices," April 2013, https://online.wsj.com/public/resources/documents/SalzReview04032013.pdf.

Communicate Your Strategy

CHAPTER 18

Leading Change and Strategic Transitions

Once you have defined and tested your strategy, you must ensure that your employees understand it and agree that it's in their interests to support it. Sometimes this comes easy, but at other times, organizational change requires a more deliberate effort on your part.

If you're leading your team through a new strategy or strategic change, you'll likely get a range of responses, from "This is exactly what we need! I'm in!" to quizzical stares and tight-lipped smiles. Some employees may respond with open doubt, fear, or anger. Too often, these reactions take managers by surprise. To ensure

---

Adapted from *Harvard Business Review Manager's Handbook* (product #10004), Harvard Business Review Press, 2017.

that your employees fully understand the change and get on board with it, you must communicate a clear vision and overcome any resistance that may occur.

Articulate a Vision That Others Will Follow

David Bradford and Allen Cohen, both scholars of business leadership, have observed that significant change only happens when someone presents a compelling vision to draw out and channel the group's energy. "People need to see that change will be worth all the effort," they write in their book *Power Up*. "It is difficult to visualize interactive changes in the abstract."

Think of a vision as a picture of the hoped-for end result of your new strategy: what it will look like, how it will function, what it will produce. It also helps to tie into something your followers already innately care about. To share that vision in a way that encourages buy-in:

Focus on people

"A vision always goes beyond the numbers that are typically found in five-year plans," says John Kotter, a professor at Harvard Business School and author of the classic book *Leading Change: Why Transformation Efforts Fail.* To reach your team at an emotional level, he suggests, tell a story about how the change you're seeking will affect real people connected with your company—customers *and* employees. Draw this picture in some detail: For example, what will an improved customer interaction look like? How will the customer and the employee feel during these interactions, and how will it

THREE KEY ASPECTS OF COMMUNICATING STRATEGY

by Georgia Everse

Not all messages are created equal. They need to be prioritized and sequenced based on their purpose. I suggest using an inspire/educate/reinforce framework as you communicate with your team and employees about strategy:

Inspire

Messages that inspire are particularly important when you are sharing a significant accomplishment or introducing a new initiative that relates to your strategy. The content should demonstrate progress against goals, showcase benefits to customers, and be presented in a way that gets attention and signals importance. The medium is less important than the impression that you leave with employees about the company. Whether you're looking to build optimism, change focus, instill curiosity, or prepare them for future decisions, you'll have more impact if you stir some emotion and create a lasting memory.

Educate

Once you've energized your team with inspiring messages, your explanations of the company's strategic decisions and your plans for implementing them

(continued)

THREE KEY ASPECTS OF
COMMUNICATING STRATEGY

should carry more weight. To educate your teams most effectively on the validity of your strategy and their role in successful execution, make sure you provide job-specific tools with detailed data that they can customize and apply in their day-to-day responsibilities. It is most important for these messages to be delivered through dialogues, rather than monologues, in smaller group sessions where employees can build to their own conclusions and feel ownership in how to implement.

Reinforce

It isn't enough to explain the connection between your company's purpose and its strategy—and between that strategy and its execution—once. You'll need to repeat the message in order to increase understanding, instill belief, and lead to true change over time. These reinforcing messages need to come in a variety of tactics, channels, and experiences. Ultimately, they serve to immerse employees in important content and give them the knowledge to confidently connect to the strategy. You'll also want to integrate these messages with your training and your human resource initiatives to connect them with employee development and performance metrics. Recognize and reward individuals and teams who come up with smart solutions and positive change.

Georgia Everse is a communications and marketing executive with 30 years of experience and a proven track record of finding innovative solutions to complex business problems. She specializes in helping C-level executives find and articulate their vision and successfully use strategic communication to achieve their growth goals. Everse is a visiting professor for the Ferris State University MBA program, in Design and Innovation Management. She is currently a partner with Genesis Inc., a brand, strategy, and communications consultancy.

Adapted from "Eight Ways to Communicate Your Strategy More Effectively" on hbr.org, August 22, 2011 (product #H007MJ).

make their lives better? The sidebar "Three Key Aspects of Communicating Strategy" provides more ways to connect with and convince your employees.

Practice, practice, practice

You probably won't get your vision statement right the first time. As you gain more experience with the change process and learn about your people's responses, modulate your pitch. Kotter offers this benchmark: "If you can't communicate the vision to someone in five minutes or less and get a reaction that signifies both understanding and interest, you are not yet done."

Weave your vision into everyday management

Your employees need repeated exposure to your ideas in order to really internalize them. "Executives who communicate well incorporate messages into their hour-by-hour activities," says Kotter. "In a routine discussion about a business problem, they talk about how proposed solutions fit (or don't fit) into the bigger picture. In a regular performance appraisal, they talk about how the employee's behavior helps or undermines the vision." By orienting employee interactions around your vision, you show your people how the strategic change will work and why it matters—and that you want them to take it seriously.

Find the right allies

People must accept the messenger before they accept the message. Chances are you aren't that messenger for everyone, and that's OK. Find people who are. Look up and down the chain of command for individuals whose colleagues see them as trustworthy and competent, and who themselves seem open to change. Focus on persuading these people, and ask them to play a leadership role with their peers. That could mean facilitating a meeting with the rest of the team, playing backup for you in a Q&A, or simply supporting your plan in regular interactions with their colleagues.

Court the uncommitted

Ronald Heifetz and Marty Linsky, who teach leadership at the John F. Kennedy School of Government at Harvard University and are in private practice with Cambridge Leadership Associates, advise that "the people who will determine your success are often those in the middle." These employees don't have anything against your initiative per se, but "they do have a stake in the comfort, stability, and security of the status quo," Heifetz and Linsky write in their *Harvard Business Review* article, "A Survival Guide for Leaders." "They've seen change agents come and go, and they know that your initiative will disrupt their lives and make their futures uncertain. You want to be sure that this general uneasiness doesn't evolve into a move to push you aside."

To recruit these players, sincerely acknowledge their accomplishments, as well as the loss and sacrifice that change entails. Help them understand the personal upside to adapting to change. Also make it clear that only those who can and will adapt will have a future on your team.

Overcome Resistance

Even if you take all these steps to gain support for your vision, your team members may still have some legitimate reservations. If you're asking them to do something new, they may worry about risking failure or about changing their status from master to apprentice. Perhaps you're asking them to throw out comfortable assumptions—that they provide a certain kind of value to the company, that the work they do is stable and prosperous. (See the sidebar "Cultivate Emotional Steadiness in Times of Change.") Maybe change upends the established balance of power, bringing some skill sets and experiences to new prominence and devaluing others.

CULTIVATE EMOTIONAL STEADINESS IN TIMES OF CHANGE

by Lisa Lai

Strategic ambiguity pushes you out of your comfort zone. When strategies shift, or are hinting toward a shift, it's normal to feel unsettled, and you'll see this in your team too. Here are three steps you can take to help yourself and your team navigate the emotions of strategic ambiguity.

Be Proactive. Learn More.

In times of change, questions arise naturally: How will this impact my group? What if everything we're doing today alters? What if this involves job changes, layoffs, or lost resources? Learn as much as you can so you're informed, not just reacting to rumor and innuendo. Use your internal network and ask others in the organization for insight, context, and clarity. When you've done the hard work of sense-making, you'll be able to anticipate the questions your team will ask and prepare the most effective answers you can.

Acknowledge and Navigate Your Own Emotions

Emotional steadiness requires that you be intentional about the way you show up in the workplace. Your role is to be calm, transparent, and steady, all while painting a vision for the future. Acknowledge your emotions and talk to a peer or your boss if you need to work through them. Play out the worst-case scenario in your mind and then move on to the more likely outcome. Chances are the reality isn't as bad as what you might conjure up when your emotions are heightened. Commit to avoiding stress responses, frustration, rumors, or other nonproductive behavior. Your team members are watching and taking their cues from you.

Keep Team Communication Open

Strategic uncertainty can cause managers to communicate with team members less frequently and less openly. "If I don't have clarity to provide, why not wait?" the thinking goes. But in truth, ambiguous situations require you to communicate even more than normal. To demonstrate emotional steadiness, share your own emotions and acknowledge those of your team in productive ways. Let team members know that what they feel is OK. But talk with them about your commitment to being emotionally steady even during times of uncertainty. Ask them to do the same and come to you if they are frustrated or concerned. Maintaining open dialogue will keep your team engaged and aligned until a clear direction emerges.

Lisa Lai serves as an adviser, consultant, and coach for some of the world's most successful leaders and companies. She is also a moderator of global leadership development programs for Harvard Business School Publishing. Find her on Facebook @Lai Ventures, follow her on Twitter @soul4breakfast, read her at soulforbreakfast.com, or visit her website at www.laiventures.com.

Adapted from "Managing When the Future Is Unclear" on hbr.org, January 9, 2019 (product #H04QGH).

Dealing with these reactions is tough, but your leadership can survive some discontent. Here are two approaches you can try:

Cook the conflict

While it's important to confront the fear and doubt that's driving resistance, you can't always afford to bring conflict to a head. Sometimes, open clashes can help resolve disagreements and channel your people's passion in a constructive way. Other times, they simply put too much stress on the group's morale.

To balance this delicate equation, Heifetz and Linsky recommend two techniques: "First, create a secure place where the conflicts can freely bubble up"—maybe an off-site retreat with an outside facilitator or an on-site conversation governed by a special set of rules for respectful, open dialogue. Insulate these conversations from your discussions about actually implementing and executing change. That means holding separate meetings, at separate times, with separate agendas. "Second, control the temperature" of the conflict by pushing people to tackle a tough issue when you think they can resolve it constructively and by backing away from disagreements or slowing the pace of change when the group's morale becomes fragile.

Engage others in problem solving

When everyone is looking to you for answers, you may feel you need to provide them all yourself. But your employees must own this change, too, and they need to feel competent in the new regime. That means "forc[ing] yourself to transfer . . . much of the work and problem-solving to others," say Heifetz and Linsky. If ever there was a time to delegate, it's now. Encourage discussion, collaboration, and creative thinking among team members around specific problems or challenges that arise.

Change management is an important skill in today's business world, where strategy-formulation initiatives, reorganizations, and audacious goals are increasingly the norm. If you lead your team through change successfully—at any level—you'll increase the group's productivity and deliver new benefits to your organization.

CHAPTER 19

Explain Your New Strategy by Emphasizing What It Isn't

by Nick Tasler

It is nearly impossible to translate—let alone *execute*—a strategy that you don't understand. Yet, according to research by MIT's Donald Sull, almost half of top executives cannot connect the dots between their company's strategic priorities, and two out of three middle managers say they simply do not understand their strategic direction.[1] McKinsey & Company reported similar findings

---

Adapted from content posted on hbr.org, May 18, 2015 (product #H022EB).

from its Organizational Health Index, as did Timothy Devinney at Australia's University of Technology in a recent experiment.[2] Taken together, this research points to the fact that most leaders just don't *get* what their organizations are trying to do.

As bleak as that sounds, leaders can avoid the problem by borrowing a technique from teachers: "compare and contrast." As educational researchers have found, it is perhaps the single best way to teach new concepts.[3]

Here's how it works. Say you're trying to teach a child what a rectangle is. It would be a mistake to only show the child a red plastic rectangle and identify it as a rectangle, because she might erroneously assume that all rectangles must be red or that color is related to shape.

So you'd need to make finer distinctions. The best approach would be to teach the child that a yellow book and a white window frame are also rectangles (compare), whereas a red ball and a maroon can of beans are *not* rectangles (contrast). As a result, our burgeoning geometry student should be able to generalize that understanding to new situations. She'll easily identify a television as a rectangle, but not a car tire—even though you never said anything about TVs or tires. She *gets* it.

Psychologists have found that the same type of compare and contrast technique is also a superior method for teaching adults how to apply abstract business principles to new situations like complex negotiations.[4]

For example, if you wanted to explain something like the "foot in the door" sales technique to a business school student, your best bet would be to describe how a door-to-door vacuum salesman begins a sales call by re-

questing permission to examine the homemaker's clean-
ing products before making the much bigger request
to purchase a vacuum cleaner. Then ask the student to
"compare and contrast" the vacuum salesman's approach
with a peace negotiator's tactic of asking for a small and
relatively unimportant parcel of land before requesting a
large payment of reparations. By doing so, the students
will grasp the general principle behind the "foot in the
door" technique, and in the future they'll be able to apply the same principle to completely new situations like
business mergers or salary negotiations.

Isn't that exactly what a strategy should do—help
teams and leaders decide the right thing to do in the face
of new threats and opportunities?

The problem is that most widely used planning processes like management by objectives and balanced
scorecards overlook the *contrast* piece of the compare-
and-contrast equation. They do a fine job of requiring
leaders to spell out what the strategic objectives *are*, but
they rarely require leaders to get clear about what they
are *not*. As a result, most leaders score a C- in strategy
comprehension.

Does this sound familiar? If it does, I would suggest
adding a wait list to your planning process—a list of objectives that you'll put on hold for three to six months.

Let's assume your planning process has revealed a list
of key growth drivers including the launch of next generation product lines, enhancing the quality of existing
products, boosting employee engagement, cutting costs,
tightening up the supply chain, and many others. Before
your team jumps into divide-and-conquer mode where

everyone lists all the ways they can contribute to those priorities, first discuss which of those priorities should go on your wait list. Even though all these priority initiatives will impact your profitable growth this year, challenge yourself and your team to put at least half of them on a wait list for three to six months.

This isn't just about trimming your list of projects. Evaluating top priorities side by side to make mutually exclusive, now-or-later distinctions will encourage your team to use comparative learning. If your team puts *launching next generation product line* on the wait list, but leaves *enhance quality of existing products* on the list of near-term priorities, that contrast makes an invaluable distinction. You have suddenly clarified that even though your team or organization absolutely values innovation, this year's strategy is actually focused more on innovating the core product lines rather than the new products. This is a subtle but important nuance.

This is precisely what Howard Schultz achieved in 2008 when he pulled Starbucks's highly profitable breakfast sandwiches from store shelves for nine months. By doing so, he instantly clarified for board members and baristas alike exactly what he meant with the new strategy of "reasserting our *coffee* authority." By pulling back on breakfast sandwiches while doubling down on research and development of new coffee creations, he engaged the whole organization in comparative learning. Everyone suddenly understood that all sources of revenue were not equal in this strategy. It clarified for store managers that "because it makes money" was not justification for straying from the coffee core.

You can accomplish the same thing with wait lists. Slowly but surely, through this repeated act of comparing and contrasting top priorities, a common theme will begin to emerge. In the minds of your team members, the hodgepodge list of projects begins taking shape as a bona fide strategy. All of the sudden, they *get* it.

To be sure, execution will always be a multifaceted beast. No one trick or tool will tame it. But a wait list can give your team a much better grip on the reins.

Nick Tasler is an organizational psychologist, author, and speaker. Connect with him at NickTasler.com; follow him on Twitter @NickTasler.

NOTES

1. Donald Sull, Rebecca Homkes, and Charles Sull, "Why Strategy Execution Unravels—and What to Do About It," *Harvard Business Review*, March 2015 (product #R1503C).

2. Arne Gast and Michele Zanini, "The Social Side of Strategy," *McKinsey Quarterly*, May 2012, https://www.mckinsey.com/business-functions/strategy-and-corporate-finance/our-insights/the-social-side-of-strategy; Timothy Devinney, "All Talk, No Action: Why Company Strategy Often Falls on Deaf Ears," *The Conversation*, March 25, 2013, https://theconversation.com/all-talk-no-action-why-company-strategy-often-falls-on-deaf-ears-12788.

3. Robert J. Marzano, Debra J. Pickering, and Jane E. Pollock, *Classroom Instruction That Works* (Alexandria, VA: Association for Supervision and Curriculum, 2001).

4. Simone Moran, Yoella Bereby-Meyer, and Max Bazerman, "Stretching the Effectiveness of Analogical Training in Negotiations: Teaching Diverse Principles for Creating Value," *Negotiation and Conflict Management Research* 1, no. 2 (2008): 99–134.

CHAPTER 20

Discussing Strategy Across Cultures

by Leonard M. Fuld

I can't stand it when someone writes "obviously" at the beginning of a sentence. Nothing is obvious to everyone, especially when it comes to appreciating the impact a person's culture has on interpreting—or preventing the acceptance of—information.

A case in point: I facilitated an important global marketing meeting in Beijing not long ago with a U.S.-based multinational food company, which had just purchased a specialty food product line from one of its rivals. The

Adapted from "Cross-Cultural Communication Takes More Than Manners" on hbr.org, August 1, 2012 (product #H0096J).

newly adopted subsidiary had recently become a market leader under its old ownership, based mostly on very good market research that was informed and driven by a deep cultural understanding of the habits and behavioral preferences of the average urban Chinese.

The new owners sent their U.S. team to participate in a strategy session, a discussion of where this Chinese subsidiary believed its market was heading and how it must respond to new and mounting competitive threats. The U.S. team set about asking questions as they would do in any meeting in the United States. They tried to be sensitive to their hosts and believed they were treading lightly. To their surprise, the Chinese nationals reacted defensively to even the smallest and seemingly most innocent questions. "Who were these 'outsiders' telling us about our market?" In essence, perhaps without recognizing it, the Americans slighted them without even knowing how or why.

It turned out that their Chinese hosts relied on close customer proximity in developing the company's packaging and marketing practices. So when the Americans suggested that perhaps their new Chinese colleagues may have overlooked new competitive threats from other multinationals as well as from home-grown rivals, the local executives viewed it as a challenge to their research and felt insulted. Interestingly, also attending were a handful of Hong Kong Chinese who were not at all upset by the Americans' questions. It turned out that many of them were educated abroad, including in the United States, and appreciated the purpose and directness of the questions posed by the U.S. execs. No harm, no foul, they felt.

At the end of the first day of meetings, the overall group accomplished little. The room felt like a boxing arena with each contingent remaining in its own corner. The Americans remained concerned over ominous signs that the company's Chinese market was about to change. Looming new government regulations would likely curb nutritional claims and impose stricter enforcement on violators. New rivals were poised to enter the market. Nevertheless, the local PRC nationals (not the Hong Kong group) remained stalwart, unconvinced that they might have to alter their existing plans. There was data to validate the Americans' concerns. Unfortunately, their very presence interfered with discussion of the issues.

On the second day, the meeting's facilitators deliberately blended the groups, and a thaw occurred in the room. The Hong Kong participants assumed the role of cultural translators and explained to their colleagues from the United States as well as the China mainlanders that each had a legitimate perspective, grounded in different methods of validation. The Chinese preferred to test their view deductively. By starting with an understanding of the cultural habits and behaviors of their customers, the Chinese team believed they could explain past, present, and future outcomes. The Westerners preferred to validate their view inductively, discovering the facts and then developing an explanatory storyline.

While the various groups still reserved their right to disagree, the session ended with something of a consensus. The local Chinese group remained determined to focus on its rigorous marketing plans, still largely driven by a series of cultural insights they had identified. At the same time, the group did concede that perhaps it needed to examine the new competition more closely and more directly. It also acknowledged a need to monitor rumors of government regulatory changes in its market.

There is nothing new about the tensions and difficulties that emerge from an intermingling of cross-cultural, cross-functional groups. While the business world is certainly far more interconnected today than it was when I started working, it nonetheless remains fraught with many land mines. Companies that have partners overseas are confronted with such talent challenges on a regular basis. Often, players from across the globe have become participants in the same enterprise, shuffled together like a deck of playing cards. But unlike perfectly uniform playing cards, people can't be so easily blended with each other.

The very richness that global yet diversified talent brings to a company can also impede its progress all because of cultural misperceptions or unintended affronts. Absorbing the strategic insights and the intelligence that drive any business decision or strategy requires awareness and the need for discussions prior to a formal meeting; the use of intermediaries such as cultural interpreters may prove useful if only to bring to the surface deeply held beliefs and assumptions.

Could we have headed off the initial locking of horns between the Americans and the mainland Chinese? Perhaps, though we were not given any warning of the prevailing temperament of both sides. More to the point, even in a world of globalization there remains an ever-present need for executives to anticipate and appreciate this frequently hidden culture factor and early on to place it on both the written and unwritten agenda of every similar meeting in the days ahead. If not, decision makers may overlook basic data—and miss major strategic opportunities.

Leonard M. Fuld is founder and principal of The Intelligent Nonprofit, a consultancy that helps nonprofits improve their strategies through its workshops and advisory services. His most recent book is *The Secret Language of Competitive Intelligence.*

Execute the Strategy and Learn from It

CHAPTER 21

Your Strategy Should Be a Hypothesis You Constantly Adjust

by Amy C. Edmondson and Paul J. Verdin

The widely accepted view that strategy and execution are separable activities sets companies up for failure in a fast-paced world.

One of us (Paul) is a strategy scholar and economist; the other (Amy) studies organizational behavior and operations management. We came together to consider why strategy so often breaks down in the execution

Adapted from content posted on hbr.org, November 9, 2017 (product #H03ZX9).

stage. While conducting research on recent dramatic cases of strategic failure in different industries, involving vastly different business models and strategies, we discovered a common pattern: What started as small gaps in execution spiraled into business failures when initial strategies were not altered based on new information provided by experience. These companies' strategies were viewed by their top executives as analytically sound; performance gaps were blamed on execution.

Take the notable failure at Wells Fargo in 2016. Executives formulated a distinctive strategy of cross-selling, which had much to recommend it. Selling additional products to current customers leverages the costs of establishing those relationships in the first place, and serving more and more of their financial service needs (to grab a greater "share of wallet") is appealing, in theory. Wells Fargo was even good in implementing the strategy—up to a point.

Yet the strategy eventually hit the realities of customers' finite wallets (their spending power) and real needs.

Cementing the business failure, salespeople appeared to believe that senior managers would not tolerate underperformance and found it easier to fabricate false accounts than to report what they were learning in the field. The widespread nature of the behavior strongly suggests that the fraud was not the result of some corrupt salespeople. Rather, it points to a system set up to fail—by the pernicious combination of a fixed strategy and executives who appeared unwilling to hear bad news. (From the perspective of the senior management at many companies, missing sales targets is a failure in the execution of an analytically sound strategy.)

An alternative perspective on strategy and execution—one that we argue is more in tune with the nature of value creation in a world marked by volatility, uncertainty, complexity, and ambiguity (VUCA)—conceives of strategy as a hypothesis rather than a plan. Like all hypotheses, it starts with situation assessment and analysis—strategy's classic tools. Also like all hypotheses, it must be tested through action. With this lens, encounters with customers provide data and insights that are of ongoing interest to senior executives—vital inputs to dynamic strategy formulation. We call this approach "strategy as learning," which contrasts sharply with the view of strategy as a stable, analytically rigorous plan for execution in the market. Strategy as learning is an executive activity characterized by ongoing cycles of testing and adjusting, fueled by data that can only be obtained through execution.

Imagine if Wells Fargo had adopted a strategy-as-learning perspective. Its top managers would have taken repeated instances of missed targets or false accounts as data to help them assess the efficacy of the cross-selling strategy. This learning would then have triggered a much-needed adjustment of the original hypothesis.

The key indicator of a strategy-as-learning approach lies in how managers interpret early signs of gaps between results and plans. Are they seen as evidence that people are underperforming? Or as data that indicates the initial assumptions were flawed, triggering further tests?

Volkswagen's software that allowed diesel engines in its vehicles to cheat on emissions tests is another case of a top-down fixed strategy that suffered in implementation. VW's strategic ambition to become the largest car company in the world required it to conquer the U.S. market. To help VW stand out and win in the U.S. market, its executives formulated a strategy of developing so-called clean-diesel vehicles that leveraged the company's core competence.

As was the case at Wells Fargo, VW's culture—specifically, its executives' lack of tolerance for pushback from people lower in the organization—seems to have played a major role in its diesel-emissions fiasco. Bob Lutz, who held leadership roles at General Motors, BMW, Ford, and Chrysler, describes a "reign of terror" that had long prevailed at VW.[1] This, he says, undoubtedly contributed to VW's ignoring evidence that the claim that the diesel technology could comply with environmental regulations was too good to be true. In this way, VW leaders lost out on the opportunity to revisit and update the strategy. Meanwhile, engineers had developed software to fool the regulators—postponing the inevitable.

Cheating and cover-ups are natural byproducts of a top-down culture that does not accept "no" or "it can't be done" for an answer. But combining this with the approach that treats strategy and execution as separable is a sure recipe for failure. At both Wells Fargo and VW, disconfirming data was available for a surprisingly long time and was not acted on by senior management. Signs that corners were being cut were ignored. And the illusion that brilliant top-down strategies were working persisted—for a time.

We are not saying top-down fixed strategies necessarily lead to fraud. Rather, our point is that these two visible examples of strategic failure illuminate the risks of failing to *integrate* strategy and execution through a deliberate and continual executive-learning process.

Strategy as learning requires senior executives to engage in an ongoing dialogue with operations across all levels and departments. The people who create and deliver products and services for customers are privy to the most important strategic data the company has available. And the strategic learning process involves actively seeking deviations that challenge assumptions underpinning current strategy. Deviations and surprises must be welcomed for their informative value in adapting the strategy. Executives who adopt a strategy-as-learning framework understand that pushing harder on execution may only aggravate the problem if shortcomings are, in fact, evidence of inadequate market intelligence or flawed assumptions about the business model.

Companies that fuse strategy and execution, continually making adjustments and periodic dramatic pivots, demonstrate what strategy as learning can look like in action. Consider the steady strategic morphing of Amazon from online bookseller to global retail powerhouse. Or take ING Bank in the Netherlands, which adopted an agile approach to strategy and execution that uses "squads" as the company's "nervous system" to sense changes in customer needs and competitive realities and to give senior executives the data they need to rethink strategy and respond. These and other cases exemplify a fundamentally different (iterative) approach to strategy making.

Of course, embracing a learning approach at the top of the organization is not a new idea. What we suggest has much in common with the notion of execution as learning, which was introduced by Amy in *Harvard Business Review* some years ago.[2] Our ideas are also consistent with current work on organizational agility—defined as an ability to sense and respond quickly to changes in the environment.

What is new is the idea that closing the gap between strategy and execution may not be about better execution after all, but rather about better learning—about more dialogue between strategy and operations, a greater flow of information from customers to executives, and more experiments. In today's fast-paced world, strategy as learning must go hand in hand with execution as learning—bypassing the idea that either a strategy or the execution is flawed—to recognize that both are necessarily flawed and both are valuable sources of learning, improvement, and reinvention for sustained value creation.

The research for this article was supported by the Harvard Business School Division of Research and by the Solvay Brussels School of Economics and Management's Baillet Latour Chair in Error Management.

Amy C. Edmondson is the Novartis Professor of Leadership and Management at Harvard Business School. She is the author of *The Fearless Organization: Creating Psychological Safety in the Workplace for Learning, Innovation, and Growth* and a coauthor of *Building the Future: Big Teaming for Audacious Innovation.* **Paul J. Verdin** is the chair in strategy and organization and director of the Baillet-Latour Chair in Error Management at Solvay Brussels School of Economics & Management (ULB, B).

NOTES

1. Bob Lutz, "One Man Established the Culture That Led to VW's Emissions Scandal," *Road & Track*, November 4, 2015, https://www.roadandtrack.com/car-culture/a27197/bob-lutz-vw-diesel-fiasco/.

2. Amy C. Edmondson, "The Competitive Imperative of Learning," *Harvard Business Review*, July-August 2008 (product # R0807E).

CHAPTER 22

Your Strategy Has to Be Flexible— but So Does Your Execution

by Martin Reeves and Rodolphe Charme di Carlo

Peter Drucker said, "Plans are only good intentions unless they immediately degenerate into hard work." This and a slew of similar maxims reflect a common view of strategy execution: that it's distinct from strategy, harder to pull off than defining a strategy, and therefore more critical to success—underpinned by seemingly

Adapted from content posted on hbr.org, November 14, 2017 (product #H040FE).

indisputable virtues such as diligence, discipline, consistency, alignment, and focus. But such a simplistic view of execution can be misleading and can reduce actual impact.

In fact, several frequently observed traps result from such a view of execution:

Losing the Plot

Action plans and Gantt charts can span many pages in pursuit of precision and concreteness. But excessive complexity can undermine thoughtful execution as much as a failure to specify tactics. In the worst case, busyness can become an implicit goal or cultural norm, and the original strategic intent can be lost in a frenzy of detail and activity. Execution must be insightfully focused on the most critical aspects of a challenge, or those which unlock other critical actions. For example, if category expansion is critical to value creation in a particular strategy, plans should focus disproportionally on how to achieve this. For example, former Mars president Paul Michaels shares in *Your Strategy Needs a Strategy*: "The job of strategy for a segment leader like us is to drive category growth, and that's the thing you should be thinking about all the time."

Metric Obsession

Drucker's exhortation "What gets measured gets managed" is often invoked when approaching execution. In the sense that results count, and their quantification is desirable, it seems irrefutable. But the worst way to achieve a goal can sometimes be to pursue it directly.

For example, new drugs are not discovered by pursuing a target number of new drugs but rather by exploring new areas of chemistry and biology. It is also a mistake to restrict ourselves to managing what we can easily measure. Few would deny the importance of corporate culture, for example, even though it is not easily quantifiable. (To read more on how metrics can distract from strategy execution, flip to the next chapter.)

Planning Myopia

Emphasizing compliance with a plan can, under stable conditions, accelerate fruition of a strategy. But under the changing conditions of a nascent or recently disrupted industry, a rigid plan can become a straitjacket for the flexibility and adaptation that are required to succeed. To take a historical example, centrally-planned economies in the Eastern Bloc left no space for adaptation to even the simplest types of change, like variation in demand. This inevitably created shortages and oversupply of goods.

Missed Learning Opportunities

The value of execution can, in the simplest cases, be boiled down to the successful accomplishment of specific tasks. But where a high degree of uncertainty and change is involved, the value can instead reside in the learning that accompanies execution, whether or not the immediate outcome is successful. Consider the example of YouTube, which began as a video dating site back in 2005. The site failed to gain traction so the founders, leveraging what they learned while building the original platform, launched another version of the website focusing on sharing videos online, with significantly more success.

Tyranny of Intermediate Goals

When goals and tasks are broken down several times into lower-level ones, it can clarify what is required of an individual or department and can therefore help scale the job of execution. But often the intermediate goal or task becomes an end in itself. A famous example is Hoover's free flights promotion. In 1992, to free up warehouse space, the UK team promised free airline tickets to customers who purchased more than £100 worth of its products. A little later, the U.S. marketing team offered the same promotion to U.S. customers in order to boost sales. The offer was implemented so "successfully" that the company could meet neither the demand for vacuum cleaners nor the cost of the flights. As a consequence, after the courts settled customer complaints, the U.S.-based company had lost £48 million and had to sell its UK branch a few years later.

Missing the Forest for the Trees

Strategic plans are often broken down into different modules for execution by different parts of an organization. Yet sometimes optimization of the parts does not lead to optimization of the whole. To take a biological example, the U.S. National Parks policy used to be to extinguish all forest fires. This led to an increase in the severity of fires. Why? Because most fires are small and stop by themselves, while creating natural firebreaks and eliminating the undergrowth that can fuel larger fires. In 1972, the policy was therefore adjusted so that only man-made fires were fought.

Businesses can be equally complex: A diversity initiative, for example, might include some compulsory training, but if this triggers sentiments of resistance and skepticism, it can be self-defeating. Every action can change perceptions, motivations, and actions, such that a list of individually plausible actions can easily create the opposite of the intended effect. In such cases, a holistic perspective to strategy and execution is required.

Execution as a Thing

We often treat strategy and execution as being separable disciplines, each with its own distinct and constant character. But as we have shown in *Your Strategy Needs a Strategy*, different strategic environments require different approaches to strategy and execution. A nascent technology business might require an adaptive approach and a stable commodity business might require a classical, planning-based approach. In predictable classical environments, strategy formulation can be separated from execution. But in adaptive environments, it cannot, since "strategy" continually emergences from amplifying the results of success experiments, i.e., execution. Furthermore, the nature of execution is also very different for each case. In the first, it centers on compliance to a predetermined plan; in the latter, on decentralized initiative taking and experimentation.

Tyranny of Practicality

That an execution plan be "practical"—simple, concrete, familiar, and unchanging—seems incontrovertible. Execution is praxis, after all. But when dealing with new or changing situations, familiar, plausible actions can easily fail to achieve the desired effect. Polaroid, for example, was a pioneer in digital photography. Yet, it tried to sell its digital cameras using the same business model as its film-based cameras—by aiming to make high margins on instant film sales. Believing that users would want hard copies, it added digital technology to instant cameras instead of creating a new product not requiring film. As we now know, the company lost to rivals. Former Polaroid CEO Gary T. DiCamillo summarizes the company's failure well: "The reason we couldn't stop the engine was that instant film was the core of the financial model of this company."[1] More broadly, a mature business can often create its own increasingly questionable reality by focusing on the part of the market where its own beliefs about how things work still apply, creating a double opportunity for disrupters—one physical and one mental. Indeed, entrepreneurs and disrupters often refer to this double inertia of incumbents as their greatest asset in taking on incumbents.

We should not let the simplistic but comforting dualism of strategy and execution deceive us. Execution should be as varied, as thoughtful, as subtle, as diverse, and as intertwined with strategy as is necessary to get the job done, and that will vary according to the specific challenge at hand. In short, your execution needs a strategy.

———————

Martin Reeves is a senior partner and managing director in the Boston Consulting Group's San Francisco office and the chairman of the BCG Henderson Institute. He is the coauthor of *Your Strategy Needs a Strategy* (Harvard Business Review Press, 2015). Follow him on Twitter @MartinKReeves. **Rodolphe Charme di Carlo** is a project leader in the Boston Consulting Group and an ambassador to the BCG Henderson Institute.

NOTE

1. Andrea Nagy Smith, "What Was Polaroid Thinking?" *Yale Insights*, November 4, 2009, https://insights.som.yale.edu/insights/what-was-polaroid-thinking.

CHAPTER 23

Stop Letting Quarterly Numbers Dictate Your Strategy

by David Hersh

In 2008, as the CEO of a software company that had just missed its target for the second quarter in a row, I was so intent on hitting our fourth-quarter revenue number of $8 million—and so scared for my job—that I promised the company I would get a tattoo of the number somewhere on my body if we hit it.

Adapted from content posted on hbr.org, December 13, 2016 (product #H03C2S).

No single metric has more drama surrounding it than quarterly revenue. Make it, and you're a hero. Miss it, and you may not have a job. But beneath the drama lies real danger. In my experience, nothing has done more long-term damage to promising young companies than focusing on quarterly revenue.

For public companies, the issues surrounding the "beat or miss" quarterly updates are well documented. Short-term scrutiny leads to short-term moves, activist shareholder shenanigans, and other tricks used to bump up the price of the stock. These pressures distract company leaders from the company's long-term health.

But it's not just the big public companies that fall into this revenue-focus trap. I've advised hundreds of start-ups and growth companies that feel the same short-term pressure. Their boards push aggressively on quarterly sales goals. And with only six to eight board meetings a year, most outside board members don't grasp the big-picture strategy in the same way that the CEO does.

There's nothing wrong with having a quarterly target; cash is the oxygen of a growth business, and it needs to be managed very carefully. But leaders, especially those who are still learning to navigate their market, must have a deep, unwavering focus on how they will win over the long run. Doing anything else is like driving across the country while looking only five feet in front of your car.

Here's an example from an SVP of product for a once-promising $20 million software company:

We raised over $100 million in venture capital but were still figuring out a repeatable business model. We

*couldn't learn how to make the model work because
our strategic moves were always trumped by having
to make the quarterly number. The CEO we hired was
a bean counter who made the numbers reinforce his
story, and the board bought into it, but it was a false
story. The sales team was amazing, but it was too hard
to sell because the product had no more differentiation
or vision. Over time the company lost relevance in the
market, all the good people left (myself included), and
the potential acquirers were no longer interested.*

In a scenario like this one, the sales team may respond admirably to revenue pressure, but their "do whatever it takes" mentality usually leads to chaos in the name of getting deals done. The result? You push innovation aside, compromise market positioning, turn the product into a dumpster of features, and create a trail of mayhem, making these deals successful postsale. And every subsequent quarter becomes increasingly difficult.

It doesn't have to be that way.

While not every company can have a Jeff Bezos or a Steve Jobs who can keep the board focused on long-term vision, it is possible for CEOs and other leaders to have an enlightened conversation around strategy and to better manage unrealistic or misguided expectations from the board.

In table 23-1, you'll find a few "canary in the coal mine" warning signs that the number has gotten too important and advice for avoiding the situation.

If you are a CEO or senior leader and find that revenue has become shorthand for whether the business

TABLE 23-1

Are quarterly numbers becoming too important to your company?

There are warning signs to watch out for.

Warning sign	Solution
The board focuses on sales results rather than key strategic issues.	Architect board meetings around three to five important strategic issues, and reinforce the quarterly number as a result of strategy, not the other way around.
Executives, employees, and the board can't articulate the strategy.	Communication of the strategy is as important as the strategy itself, so ensure your "aggressive but achievable" plan is clear to everyone.
Your company is adding people too fast for its growth rate and market position.	It's better to do a one-off downsizing rather than sacrifice your vision and strategy with destructive, short-term cash moves, so size according to the true position of your company.
Your R&D road map is always slipping.	Ensure the R&D department has a voice in strategy and deal triage, and that the best people have a reason to stay motivated.
The sales team is only focused on commissions.	Hire a strategic head of sales who can see the big picture of business building, not just last minute heroics, and balance quota compensation with equity and other incentives.

is working, it's time to change the conversation. In my experience, these are the four main ways to drive that change:

- Ensure that your strategic plan is still appropriate, clear, and embraced by the team. It's often shocking to most leaders, but up to 95% of employees are unaware of, or don't understand, company strategy.[1] Update the plan as needed and make sure it can be summarized in a short, clear statement that employees can express with confidence and energy.

- A McKinsey study found that only 21% of board members (public and private boards) fully understand the company strategy.[2] To get past this hurdle, meet with board members individually to delve deeply into how the company plans to win, but also spend time listening to each member's motivations, ideas, concerns, and aspirations for the company. You need to build strong connective tissue between management and the board.

- Update the company dashboard around the key metrics that support the company's long-term goals, and ensure those KPIs are aligned with the company's purpose. Visually represent sales numbers as the result of strategic execution, not the goal.

- Keep the strategic communication and metrics flowing constantly, and celebrate the successes and course corrections that accelerate the strategy. Companies should be in a "flow state" where information is constantly available and is driving decision making throughout the organization.

Quarterly sales numbers are important, but they are also a deceptively comfortable way to manage a growth company. It can feel good to hit the number and pop the champagne. But leading with that number is lazy, a death knell for innovation and long-term success, and can disguise the real issues facing the company's prospects. The biggest value creation comes from companies that know how to win over the long run.

Oh, and my tattoo promise? We did hit our number that quarter. And yes, I still have Roman numeral VIII on my ankle. I'm proud of that period of time, but if I were coaching a leader or CEO foolish enough to make the same promise, I would recommend a more inspiring, strategic image. And maybe start with a temporary tattoo.

David Hersh is an entrepreneur, investor, and adviser based in San Francisco who writes about transforming startups into breakout companies. He was the founding CEO at Jive Software and now the CEO of Mobilize. Follow him on Twitter @djhersh.

NOTES

1. Robert S. Kaplan and David P. Norton, "The Office of Strategy Management, *Harvard Business Review*, October 2005 (product #R0510D).

2. Chinta Bhagat, Martin Hirt, and Conor Kehoe, "Tapping the Strategic Potential of Boards," *McKinsey Quarterly*, February 2013, https://www.mckinsey.com/business-functions/strategy-and -corporate-finance/our-insights/tapping-the-strategic-potential -of-boards.

CHAPTER 24

Strategy Is All About Practice

by Roger L. Martin

I have never seen anybody become good at strategy without practice. It may happen, but I have never seen it. I doubt that I will see it, because strategy is a discipline. Like any discipline, you have to believe in it and work at it to become skilled; both mindset and effort are required to make progress and become adept at strategy.

The key to the strategy mindset is to view business life as not entirely random; stochastic but not random. While it may be necessary to revisit and revise choices more often than convenient, the assumption holds that

---

Adapted from content posted on hbr.org, February 20, 2013 (product #H00A2N).

effortful, determined, revisable strategy is better than simply letting happen whatever will happen.

By far the easiest thing to do is to see the future as so unpredictable and uncertain that you should keep all your options open and avoid choice-making entirely. The irony, of course, is that not choosing is every bit as much a choice, and every bit as impactful, as choosing to choose.

There is a bit of F. Scott Fitzgerald here: He wrote that "one should . . . be able to see that things are hopeless yet be determined to make them otherwise." Businesses will evolve and change in ways that make last month's or last year's investment decisions look stupid. It will happen, no matter who you are or how smart you are. It happened to Warren Buffett with Salomon Brothers, Dexter Shoes, US Airways, and Conoco. But those are anomalies among the countless other bets that worked out largely as he thought they would. The mindset of a strategist is to hold that just because some bets turn out to be wrong doesn't mean that the future is entirely unpredictable.

If the first necessary element to being an accomplished strategist is belief, the second is work, work, and work some more. This means making strategy choices, seeing how they work out, and then learning from them. Strategy is part art and part science; a heuristic, not an algorithm. As with most heuristics, you can learn the categories to think about: Pay attention to customers, to competitors, to capabilities, to elements of industry evolution. But there isn't a learnable formula about how to put them together in any given choice context.

That is what requires practice—and the form of that practice is really important. In golf, you might feel that going to the driving range and hitting a thousand balls is inherently good practice. It isn't, though, if all you do is go up to the tee, pound the ball as hard as you can, and see whether it went straight and far. If some shots were great and others not so much, what did you learn? Just about nothing, unless you thought in advance about what you were trying to do and what you would pay attention to (for example, head stillness, hip turn, hands leading, etc.). And still, in golf, you probably need a swing coach to watch what you actually do, versus what you hope you are doing, in order to learn something useful.

In strategy, helpful practice means setting out your logic about a choice in advance—for example, "I think consumers will react in this way," "competitors will react that way," "we will be able to deliver this," and "we will achieve this outcome"—and then watching what actually happens against this predicted logic. This is the only way you will learn; the only way you will figure out whether your logic was entirely sound or flawed in some way.

And when I say setting out your logic, I mean writing it down in advance, not just thinking it through. That is important because of our human capacity for ex post facto rationalizing absolutely anything and everything. If you don't write down in advance what your logic was, you will find that you will convince yourself that everything worked out the way you thought it would—and you will learn nothing. In golf, your swing coach can keep you honest—no, you didn't lead with your hands through impact. But in strategy, you need to keep yourself honest.

Of course, you can't ever eliminate chance. You may have made a bet that was a sound one but didn't pay off this time because you were unlucky. Perhaps it had an 80% chance of paying off, and you fell prey to the 20%. That is why lots of practice and experience is required—they build up your repertoire of bet analysis and observation. The more you practice, the less exposed to chance you'll be—though it never quite goes away.

Bottom line: If you believe that you can succeed more often than not in dealing with the inherent uncertainty of the future and you practice at laying out your logic, making strategic choices, and assessing the outcomes, you will become an accomplished strategist.

Roger L. Martin is professor emeritus and former dean of the Rotman School of Management at the University of Toronto. He is a coauthor of *Creating Great Choices: A Leader's Guide to Integrative Thinking* (Harvard Business Review Press, 2017).

Index

Engage with HBR content the way you want, on any device.

With HBR's new subscription plans, you can access world-renowned **case studies** from Harvard Business School and receive **four free eBooks**. Download and customize prebuilt **slide decks and graphics** from our **Visual Library**. With HBR's archive, top 50 best-selling articles, and five new articles every day, HBR is more than just a magazine.

Subscribe Today
hbr.org/success

Smart advice and inspiration from a source you trust.

If you enjoyed this book and want more comprehensive guidance on essential professional skills, turn to the HBR Guides Boxed Set. Packed with the practical advice you need to succeed, this seven-volume collection provides smart answers to your most pressing work challenges, from writing more effective emails and delivering persuasive presentations to setting priorities and managing up and across.

Harvard Business Review Guides

Available in paperback or ebook format. Plus, find downloadable tools and templates to help you get started.

- Better Business Writing
- Building Your Business Case
- Buying a Small Business
- Coaching Employees
- Delivering Effective Feedback
- Finance Basics for Managers
- Getting the Mentoring You Need
- Getting the Right Work Done

- Leading Teams
- Making Every Meeting Matter
- Managing Stress at Work
- Managing Up and Across
- Negotiating
- Office Politics
- Persuasive Presentations
- Project Management

The most important management ideas all in one place.

We hope you enjoyed this book from *Harvard Business Review*. For the best ideas HBR has to offer turn to HBR's 10 Must Reads Boxed Set. From books on leadership and strategy to managing yourself and others, this 6-book collection delivers articles on the most essential business topics to help you succeed.

HBR's 10 Must Reads Series

The definitive collection of ideas and best practices on our most sought-after topics from the best minds in business.

- Change Management
- Collaboration
- Communication
- Emotional Intelligence
- Innovation
- Leadership
- Making Smart Decisions

- Managing Across Cultures
- Managing People
- Managing Yourself
- Strategic Marketing
- Strategy
- Teams
- The Essentials

hbr.org/mustreads

Buy for your team, clients, or event.
Visit hbr.org/bulksales for quantity discount rates.

Notes

Notes

Notes

Notes

Notes

Notes

Notes

Notes

Notes